KOL HAN'SHAMAH כל הנשמה

BAND VOLUME II

ARRANGEMENTS BY EMILY TUMMONS
EDITED BY JOEL EGLASH

companion volume for choir also available

TRANSCONTINENTAL
MUSIC PUBLICATIONS
A Division of the American Conference of Cantors

ABOUT YOUR RIGHT TO REPRODUCE THE MUSIC IN *Kol Han'shamah: Band Volume II*

HEBREW PRONUNCIATION GUIDE

VOWELS	CONSONANTS
a as in father	ch as in Bach or Scottish loch (not as in cheese)
ai as in aisle (= long i as in island)	g = hard g as in get (not soft g as in gem)
e as in bed	tz as in boats
ei as in eight (= long a as in ace)	h after a vowel is silent
i as in pizza (= long e as in be)	r = like the Italian (rolled) or French r
o as in go	
u as in lunar	
' = unstressed vowel close to ə or unstressed short e	

KOL HAN'SHAMAH: BAND VOLUME II

Companion volume to *Kol Han'shamah: Choir Volume II* (TMP 994068)

Proofread by Cantor Claire Franco, Dr. Alan Mason, Emily Tummons, and Josh Wiczer
Copyedited by Debra Corman – Music engraved by Josh Wiczer
Design and compositing by Joel Eglash

Transcontinental Music Publications Executive Committee:
—Joel Eglash, Cantor Lauren Phillips Fogelman, Cantor Claire Franco, and Cantor Steven Weiss
American Conference of Cantors: President, Cantor Seth Warner; COO, Rachel Roth
TMP / JLicense Customer Support: Stacey Berliner – TMP / JLicense Production Assistant: Eden Franco

Transcontinental Music Publications / JLicense
A DIVISION OF THE AMERICAN CONFERENCE OF CANTORS
The world's leading publisher of Jewish music since 1938
1375 Remington Road, Suite M – Schaumburg, IL 60173
847.781.7800 – tmp@accantors.org

Printed in the United States of America – 10 9 8 7 6 5 4 3 2 1
Item number 994069 – ISBN 979-8-9889024-2-3
Includes audio download code insert
TranscontinentalMusic.com

Funding and support for *Kol Han'shamah: Band Volume II*
was generously provided by

Hebrew Union College–Jewish Institute of Religion
Debbie Friedman School of Sacred Music Class of 2015
Cantor Ben Ellerin
Cantor Susan Lewis Friedman
Cantor Rayna Green
Cantor Sara Hass
Cantor Amanda Kleinman
Cantor Dave Malecki
Cantor Inbal Sharett-Singer

and

The Lowell Milken Fund for American Jewish Music
at the UCLA Herb Alpert School of Music

CONTENTS

Arrangements by Emily Tummons

** Piano-vocal-guitar (PVG) — ** Lead sheets include melody, lyrics, and chords; may also be used as the Melody for C Instruments part*

One of the great innovations in contemporary progressive Jewish worship is the volunteer band (and choir). These ensembles help us to find new ways for congregants to connect with their communities and to contribute *ruach* (spirit) to services. As an instrumentalist and arranger myself, I've seen firsthand how impactful these bands can be.

The music in the *Kol Han'shamah: Band* book series can be used interchangeably on its own, with a cantor or solo vocalist, or to support the choral music in the companion volume *Kol Han'shamah: Choir*, which was created to provide two-part choir arrangements of popular tunes for the synagogue volunteer choir.

The excellent arrangements in this volume were masterfully created by Emily Tummons. Emily and I worked together to produce volumes of arrangements that the amateur musician could pick up and play with minimal practice time (greatly helped by the accompanying practice track recordings) and that offer opportunities for the more experienced instrumentalist to spice things up with an optional lead solo line. The format of the parts allows for a maximum amount of interchangeable common instruments.

Please take some time, before planning your first use of the music in this book series, to read through Emily Tummons's thorough and very useful introductory material and resources, especially if you do not yet have experience leading instrumentalists or planning which parts they should play.

For their contributions to this project, thank you to Emily Tummons, Cantor Claire Franco, Cantor Steven Weiss, Dr. Alan Mason, the composers of the music in and the proofreaders of this volume, Josh Wiczer, and the staff and leadership of the ACC and Transcontinental Music Publications, including president Cantor Seth Warner, COO Rachel Roth, and Stacey Berliner. The indespensible rehearsal recordings included with this book feature Cantor Emma Lutz and Cantor Billy Tiep accompanied by Tali Tadmor and the UCLA instrumentalists listed on page xxxiv; our deepest thanks to them for their immense effort and excellent musicianship. With great thanks we acknowledge the generosity of the HUC–JIR class of 2015 and the Lowell Milken Center for Music of American Jewish Experience at UCLA. In particular, from the Milken and UCLA team, we are grateful to Dr. David Brown, Dr. Mark Kligman, Sharyl Holtzman, Jose Carrillo, and Laura Agudelo Cuartas for use of studio, engineering / mixing / mastering, and resources.

Joel Eglash
Founding Series Editor
Nisan 5784 / April 2024

It has been a joy to work alongside Joe Eglash and the rest of the *Kol Han'shamah* team, making these arrangements and writing the introductory chapters of these volumes. I hope that you who are seasoned band directors will find in these resources an abundance of fresh, practical ideas to rejuvenate the work you do with your bands and to inspire you. For leaders with less experience with band instruments, I sincerely hope these resources will make the road ahead less daunting and that you find in this volume more than enough knowledge to step into your next (or first) rehearsal season with a sense of excitement.

It's my wish that these simple band parts and the accompanying resources will open doors for more and more of our volunteer players to be welcomed into our synagogue bands with ease.

I want to thank my family and friends for their immense support to me in this undertaking, especially my partner Hunter, without whom it would not have been possible for me to devote the better part of a year to this wonderful project.

I gratefully recognize my music professors and teachers from years past and the many ways that their areas of expertise have shaped and inspired my arranging work, especially Lisa Schneider for oboe performance and music theory; Rabbi Alexandria Shuval-Weiner and Cantor Sharon Kohn for liturgical music; and my parents, Mike and Jane Tummons, for using music as a tool for building joyful, inclusive communities.

Emily Tummons
Nisan 5784 / April 2024

Emily Tummons is the Transcontinental Music Publications featured arranger for *Kol Han'shamah: Band* volumes I and II.

Her original Jewish compositions are published in the Transcontinental Music Publications songbooks *Shabbat Anthology Volume IX*, *Nigun Anthology Volume III*, *Mikraei Kodesh Volume II*, and *High Holy Days Anthology Volume II*. During her career in Jewish music, Emily has served as *t'filah* band leader and arranger, religious school music teacher, choral conductor, full-time music director, and guitar and piano accompanist for synagogues in the greater Kansas City area.

Oboe is Emily's primary instrument, and she is a long-time member of the International Double Reed Society. She is also an active supporter and past board member of the Guild of Temple Musicians, an affiliate of the American Conference of Cantors. In addition to her work in Jewish music, Emily serves on the faculty at the University of Kansas, where she completed her postgraduate studies in linguistics.

QUICK-START GUIDE

Welcome! Here is a brief rundown, for when you need to set things in motion fast. When you have some more time, read through the following pages and use them as a key resource for management of your ensemble. In it, you'll find many more details and helpful tips on topics like these:

» **What is this songbook?** *Kol Han'shamah: Band* offers new plug-and-play arrangements for volunteer synagogue bands. Its companion volume offers the same tunes, but arranged for volunteer synagogue choirs. All parts in both books are designed to be played together and are interchangeable.

» **Who can play these arrangements?** Every one of your band members, from the amateur volunteer to the professional guest musician, can play from this volume. You can use these arrangements when you have just one band member playing at a given event, when you've got dozens of players, or any number in between.

» **Refer to the Full Score** of a song to see it all, at a glance. You'll find the melody, guitar chords, Parts 1 and 2, a small-note solo option, bass, and keyboard. The pages labeled "Piano / Vocal" (following each Full Score) can be given to your keyboard player. After the Piano / Vocal part, you'll find every other individual part for that song.

» **Which part goes to which player?** The answer may depend on the skill level of your players, and not as much on which instruments they play. Here's what each part does, in a nutshell:

Part 1: Give this line, the most vital harmony line of all the options, to your strongest, best player of any treble clef instrument. If you have only one player for an event, use Part 1.

Part 2: This line is easier to play than Part 1 and is suited for less-skilled players. It works with Part 1 to fill out the rest of the harmony notes.

Small-Note Solo Option: If Part 1 is covered, consider assigning a highly skilled player to this enriching line. It contains extra flourishes and runs that are ideal for a solo instrument.

Melody: The melody is critical when playing these songs as preludes and postludes. You might decide to give players this line when a song is sung, too, depending on the overall balance.

Bass: Bass players will find here both the chord labels and a fully notated, simple bass line that helps establish the song's groove.

» **Which key is this instrument in?** In this volume all parts except the bass are made available in the three common instrument keys. Refer to the Instrumental Chart when looking up specific instruments. Below is a handy list of common examples to double-check before distributing parts:

C Instruments: cello, flute, oboe, recorders, trombone, tuba, viola, violin
B♭ Instruments: clarinet, soprano and tenor saxophones, trumpet
E♭ Instruments: alto and baritone saxophones

» **Can I legally make copies?** Yes! Please refer to the legal statement on the second page of this book. Be sure to share this book's rehearsal tracks with your players, too. Your band members will find these audio recordings to be indispensable tools for practicing.

INSTRUMENTAL CHART

—C INSTRUMENTS: These instruments will require parts labeled "... for C Instruments." Notes sound the same as written (tuba sounds an octave lower).

CATEGORY	INSTRUMENT	CLEF(S)	TUNING *To match these concert pitches:*	 *C instruments play:*
Woodwinds	**Flute**	Treble	—C	C—
	Oboe	Treble	—B♭	B♭—
	Bassoon	Treble (and tenor; not provided)	—A	A—
Brass	**Trombone**	Bass		
	Tuba	Bass		
Strings	**Violin**	Treble		
	Viola	Treble (and alto; not provided)		
	Cello	Bass, Treble (and tenor; not provided)		

—Bb INSTRUMENTS: These instruments will require parts labeled "... for B♭ Instruments." Notes sound one whole step lower than written (tenor sax sounds an octave lower).

CATEGORY	INSTRUMENT	CLEF(S)	TUNING *To match these concert pitches:*	 *Bb instruments play:*
Woodwinds	**Soprano Sax**	Treble	—C	D—
	Clarinet	Treble	—B♭	C—
	Tenor Sax	Treble	—A	B—
Brass	**Trumpet**	Treble		

—Eb INSTRUMENTS: These instruments will require parts labeled "... for E♭ Instruments." Notes sound four and ½ steps lower than written (baritone sax sounds an octave lower).

CATEGORY	INSTRUMENT	CLEF(S)	TUNING *To match these concert pitches:*	 *Eb instruments play:*
Woodwinds	**Alto Sax**	Treble	—C	A—
	Baritone Sax	Treble	—B♭	G—
			—A	F#—

Key of F French horn parts are not provided.

These introductory materials are packed with information and suggestions you can use to set your synagogue band up for success, whether you're new to directing or a seasoned veteran. First, in How to Use This Book, *we walk step-by-step through the features of this songbook. You'll find insights about the instruments in your band, advice about which part to give to which player, and many other topics. In the second section,* A Guide to Working with Your Band, *words of wisdom are shared on the themes of how to recruit new players, how to run rehearsals, how to use your band in a service, and more.*

HOW TO USE THIS BOOK

By Emily Tummons

——THE *KOL HAN'SHAMAH* SERIES

FORERUNNERS TO *KOL HAN'SHAMAH*——

In 2007, Joel Eglash created a three-volume set for Tara Publications: *T'filah Band* and *T'filah Choir*. He writes in the introduction that the band arrangements were "created with a volunteer band in mind—a band including players with multiple skill levels." The harmony lines "serve the song; not too simple, not too difficult . . . seasoned players will find originality, and 'weekend warriors' will find a challenge."

Through the experience gained in the intervening years, we saw that this approach to band arrangements adapted itself well to any particular cluster of players, from professional to amateur skill levels. *Kol Han'shamah* was created, in part, in response to these years of enthusiastic use of not only this set of volumes, but also that of TMP's *K'lei Zemer: Easy Arrangements for Synagogue Bands*, published in 2008.

This companion volume series, one book for choir, the other book for band, strives to carry forward this same vision, using a similar approach in the arranging process. Of the fifteen songs that appear in this band volume, you'll find a piece for Chanukah, songs to mark sacred moments in the life of a congregation, and songs for Shabbat and other holy days. You'll find new settings for traditional favorites alongside some pieces written in recent years. The choir volume contains those same fifteen songs with interchangeable parts across the whole set of songbooks.

THE COMPANION VOLUME, FOR CHOIRS——

Three groups of writers and arrangers served as the foundational architects of the beautiful harmonic decisions made in each of the fifteen pieces. They are composers Aaron Bensoussan, Menachem Creditor, Debbie Friedman, Elana Jagoda, Jeff Klepper and Dan Freelander, Eric Mandell, Dan Nichols and Mason Cooper, Hollis Schachner, Julie Silver, Peter Yarrow, Sol Zim, and Ehud and Sarah Zweig; keyboard arrangers Susan Lewis Friedman, Rachelle Nelson, Gregory Shifrin, and Robbie Solomon; and choral harmony arrangers David Berger, Susan Lewis Friedman, Rachelle Nelson, and Robbie Solomon.

The keyboard arrangements for these fifteen pieces are beautiful and simple. Those who arranged the choral harmonies took their cues from this harmonic tapestry under the melody (or in most cases wrote the keyboard accompaniment themselves) and took the arranging a step further, escorting the piece into new, interesting, and rich melodic and harmonic landscapes.

——THE BAND VOLUME

After *Kol Han'shamah: Choir* was completed, work began on the band volume. My job as arranger was to take these highly unique existing arrangements and write band parts that would work well, in a simple fashion, with the harmonic textures and styles that were already set in place.

The band volume that you hold in your hands contains all the pieces that you need to start your next band season off on the right foot. You'll find ten parts per song, which you can distribute to your players: Full Score, PVG, Lead Sheet / Melody for C Instruments, Melody for B♭ Instruments, Melody for E♭ Instruments, Melody for Bass Clef Instruments, Parts 1 & 2 for C Instruments, Parts 1 & 2 for B♭ Instruments, Parts 1 & 2 for E♭ Instruments, and Bass.

SHEET MUSIC FOR ACCOMPANYING INSTRUMENTS——

» FULL SCORE Band directors may find it useful to lead rehearsals from the Full Score. It contains every one of the parts at a glance, untransposed in concert key. The noteheads are small enough that keyboardists shouldn't expect to play their arrangement from the Full Score (they should be given the PVG part), but it could be useful to give pianists a copy of the Full Score so that during rehearsals they can help to reinforce any band parts if needed. The Full Score is the one spot in the band volume where you will find the English translations and Hebrew text of every song. Depending on the event you're rehearsing toward, it could be good to share the English meanings of the Hebrew text with your players.

» PIANO / VOCAL (PVG) Pianists collaborating with synagogue bands will find the keyboard arrangements straightforward and accessible, yet distinctive and rich. The keyboard arrangers for *Kol Han'shamah* have largely shaped the personality, style, and colors of the songs with their harmonic adaptations. The custom-written piano lines have been rigorously tested for smoothness and playability. Note that this PVG part is identical to the melody and keyboard arrangement that appears in the choir volume.

» LEAD SHEET (WITH MELODY FOR C INSTRUMENTS) Your guitarists and other plucked string instrumentalists (e.g., mandolinists) should be given the Lead Sheet, which doubles as Melody for C Instruments. This may also be what your percussionists are most comfortable playing from. The guitar chords labeled across the melody line, in both PVG and the Lead Sheet, are not simplified chords. In most cases, these chords represent the exact chord progressions written by the keyboard arrangers, chord progressions unique to this set of songbooks. If your accompanying guitarists or pianists are accustomed to playing Nelson's "Bar'chu" or Silver's "Shir Chadash" out of *The Complete Shireinu*, for example, let them know these arrangements are new and innovative! All the players in your rhythm section are encouraged to lean in fully to these arrangements, with confidence that all the parts will sound great when brought together.

» BASS The approach taken in arranging the bass lines for these fifteen songs, like the approach taken with all parts, was one of simplicity. We wanted your bassist (whether electric bass guitarist or double bass player) to be able to walk into the rehearsal right before a service and sight-read this notated part with some ease. Guitar chords are printed in the bass part as well. While some bass players may opt to do their own thing, following the chords, bass guitarists are encouraged to take full advantage of these arranged lines. They are custom-built for this volume. In the process of arranging, attention was given to what the left hand does in the keyboard arrangements of each song, taking cues from that groove, and working hand in hand with it to make a solid yet simple bass part. When you do not have a bass player for a service, the bass line could be given instead to a tuba player, to favorable effect. Or, try experimenting with other lower-register instruments, depending on the overall balance of your ensemble: bassoon, bass clarinet, bass trombone, cello, (left-hand) synthesizer, or baritone saxophone.

SHEET MUSIC FOR BAND INSTRUMENTS——

The most unique offering of this band volume is the arrangement of simple harmony counterpoint lines that band players of most skill levels can play. You do not have to be a professional musician to play these parts well! Three harmony lines are provided (Part 1, Part 2, and a small-note solo option), in the three common instrument keys (C, B♭, and E♭), for each of the fifteen pieces. These three all appear together on the page, to give maximum flexibility to the director and players. Here's a snapshot of what each of the three parts does:

» PART I Part 1 is Priority 1. This part hands over to us the most vital harmony line of all the options offered. In settings when you only have one instrument player, give him or her this line, rather than Part 2 or the small-note solo option. In Part 1, we find the richest harmony paths that a single volunteer band player could take, similar to a classic tenor line in SATB choral music. It's more complex, interesting, and challenging than Part 2; even so, it's designed to be playable by amateur musicians.

» PART 2 This is an optional instrumental harmony part. It shouldn't be played at all in cases where there's only one instrumentalist: if Part 1 will be solidly handled, placing one or more players on Part 2 will help you fill out the rest of the harmony in each of the fifteen pieces. Part 2 plays a role that is not unlike the alto's role in a conventional SATB choral arrangement. Parts 1 and 2 fit together like a hand in glove. In Part 2, we find harmony lines that are easier to play than the ones we find in Part 1. Part 2 is the most accessible, out of all the band parts, for musicians who are not professionals.

» SMALL-NOTE SOLO OPTION Along the top of the staff for Part 1, you will often find an optional solo instrument line with small noteheads. These lines contain flourishes and runs that are going to add richness to the piece. These embellishments may be above the average technical ability of "weekend warrior" players. This small-note option harmony line is layered into this songbook for those moments of the year when you may have a highly skilled player joining your team. Give this line to that solo instrument only if Part 1 will also be covered.

» MELODY In this volume, the melody line is provided as its own part that can be assigned to an instrument. You'll find it for C instruments in treble clef (shared with the Lead Sheet) and bass clef, for B♭ instruments, and for E♭ instruments. Parts 1 and 2, and at times the small-note option, take turns weaving in and out of heavy, frequent reinforcement of the melody in every piece. Because of this, in many cases, directors may not need to assign the melody line to any players. But if you have extra players, or if there are other reasons the melody line calls out for reinforcement in your particular service or event, you'll find melody for C (both treble and bass clefs), B♭, and E♭ instruments.

The melody line throughout this volume is not necessarily by default the easiest of all the lines to play. As band directors, we shouldn't assume that we can hand the melody over to our less-skilled players and expect it to be more easily mastered than Part 2. You may also notice moments of songs when it doesn't make sense to have the melody played on a band instrument while it is being sung (e.g., the first few bars of section C in "Bar'chu," the first few bars of section F in "L'chah Dodi," etc.); so when in doubt, cut. On the other hand, the melody line is critical for use in instrumental preludes and postludes.

REPRODUCTION OF PARTS——

Now that you've purchased this volume, the arrangements are licensed for the use of your synagogue or group. Make or distribute whatever copies you need for your players—any part, any song. Photocopying and dissemination of digital files is permitted with the purchase of this book; you don't have to buy any individual pieces or parts or additional copies.

You might also distribute the Instrumental Chart to tuck into the front pockets of your leader binders. This could include giving one to your pianist, section leaders, or anyone who aids in the process of tuning the ensemble. Be sure to share this volume's rehearsal tracks with your players, too. Your band members will find the audio recordings to be indispensable tools as they practice!

THE REHEARSAL TRACK RECORDINGS——

The rehearsal tracks provided with *Kol Han'shamah* will be supremely useful in getting your players prepared and ready. For each of the songs, you'll find tracks that spotlight each of the parts—tracks that give your players the support and targeted practice they'll need. The following instruments were selected for the production of this volume's rehearsal tracks alongside bass, keyboard, and singers:

Part 1: clarinet Part 2: trumpet Small-Note Solo Option: violin

» FIRST AUDIO TRACK The first track for each song in your bundle of recordings provides everything, all together. You'll hear piano, bass, Parts 1 and 2, and the optional small-note solo instrument, in addition to the voices from the corresponding arrangement in *Kol Han'shamah: Choir*. This is a great tool for experiencing how all of the pieces of the puzzle fit together, reinforcing and complementing each other. This is the only track where the small-note solo instrument line can be heard.

» SECOND AUDIO TRACK Share this track with those in your band who will be playing Part 1, the primary harmony line. In this track #2, the keyboard, bass, and Part 2 are all set at a lower volume, in the background. It is Part 1 that can be heard the best, in the foreground. No voices are included.

» THIRD AUDIO TRACK Share this track with those in your band who will be playing Part 2, the easier harmony line. In this track #3, the keyboard, bass, and Part 1 are all set at a lower volume, in the background—it is Part 2 that can be most prominently heard. Again, no voices are included.

» FOURTH AUDIO TRACK Share this track with a skilled instrumentalist in your band who will be playing the optional small-note solo line. Again, no voices are included.

——KEY FEATURES OF THE BAND ARRANGEMENTS

These arrangements were designed to help volunteer bands sound the best that they can! The parts are simple, straightforward, and very much in sync with every other moving piece in the broader ensemble. Keeping things simple elevates the sound of "weekend warriors" who don't play professionally. It also elevates the sound of better-skilled ensembles who are short on practice time.

Below, some of the facets of Parts 1 and 2 are described, along with the concrete ways these lines were kept clean, solid, and playable. These facets do not apply as much to the small-note solo option, since that's written for a more technically skilled single player.

THE INS AND OUTS——

» RHYTHM Busy, cluttered rhythms were avoided as much as possible for Parts 1 and 2 (e.g., unexpected syncopation). Those who play these lines will rarely play anything faster than an eighth note. In the scattered few spots with sixteenth notes, it's a special moment that is reinforced rhythmically by other players, or it's reinforcing a strong phrase in the melody. Relative rhythms are smooth too. The rhythms in Parts 1 and 2 tend to be in alignment with the keyboard, melody, small-note solo option, or choir harmony. No surprise rhythms and no rhythms that go against the grain of another player's rhythm are included. For example, there are no triplets in contrast to another player's quarter notes, even though objectively a technique like that could make for interesting arranging.

» PITCH AND RANGE In general, players who are not professional musicians will sound the best in the middle areas of their ranges. Things can get really tough for them out at the extreme ends of their instrument's range, so we tried to avoid those outer edges. Players of any skill level, but especially amateur players, sound their best when they stick to a conservative middle range of pitches for their instruments. These arrangements reflect that. Part 2, the lowest of the three band parts, never ventures below a concert C just below the treble clef staff (C3). The small-note solo option, the highest of the three band parts, never ventures above a concert C just above the treble clef staff (C5).

Attention was given to relative pitches as well. We kept the intervals between notes modest in size—a big leap from one note over to the next is scarce in these arrangements. Also, voice crossing is almost never used. This means Part 1 is nearly always higher than Part 2. And the small-note solo option is almost always higher than Part 1. One benefit of avoiding voice crossing is that less-experienced players can keep better track of where they are in the overall blend, where their part falls relative to another player near them. For volunteer musicians, avoiding voice crossing can help their resulting sound be less chaotic and more tidy.

» ARTICULATION We wanted to give your players every chance to sound smooth, not sloppy or messy. And erring on the side of more than enough overt slur markings throughout every song can work to the benefit of the amateur band. While they may not slur every note, the goal is that they avoid frequent harsh tonguing. There are very few staccato markings for Parts 1 and 2, even though there are some energetic and crisp passages in some songs. And there are no trills or other articulations that could trip up an inexperienced player; we even refrained from indicating breath marks.

Another benefit to keeping the articulations to a bare minimum is that there are so many different kinds of instruments that may be assigned to Part 1 or Part 2 for a given service. A trumpet player handles articulations in Part 1 differently from the way a violinist does when playing Part 1. The arrangements need to accommodate all of this diversity. So under-marking the nuanced articulations, along with the expanded use of slurs, helps allow for any instrument to play any part smoothly and competently and in their own way.

» DYNAMICS Our band instruments are delivering only a portion of the total sonic impact of a song. Other integral portions of the whole are delivered by the keyboardist, the bass player, and the singers. The average unamplified band instrument will be louder than the average unamplified voice. This was held in mind when marking dynamics. In general the band parts are marked at least one notch lower in volume than the voices are. So, for example, in a section where the singers have *mf*, the band players typically have *mp*. There are exceptions to this, but in general the sheet music encourages band members not to overplay, and instead to serve what is going on in the service.

» STRONG ENDINGS How we conclude a song makes a big difference in a service. Bringing intention to the final moments of a sung prayer can help the essence of that prayer settle into the hearts of the congregation, echoing over them in the moments that follow. We've shaped these arrangements so the players can really shine on the endings of the songs. If there's time during sound check, think about playing the last few bars of that service's pieces, to refresh everyone's memory and to get prepared to stick the landing together.

HOW THE PARTS INTERACT WITH THE WHOLE——

» INTERCHANGEABILITY Great care was taken in the arranging of this volume to make sure that no single part depended too much on another dimension also being played. The parts might shine the best with an all-hands-on-deck rendering of a given song: a choir singing the lines from the choir volume, a pianist playing the printed keyboard arrangement, a guitarist following the provided guitar chords, a bass guitarist playing the bass line provided, and so on. But the parts still work well even if you have only guitar accompaniment for a given service (no keyboard or bass) or if you've got just keyboard, for example. The parts were written to interlock fully, but you don't have to have 100 percent of them present in order to deliver great renditions of these pieces.

» REINFORCEMENT OF MELODY We have often arranged Parts 1 and 2 so that one or the other of them will reinforce the melody, either in an exact way or in a simple way that is a broad nod to the melody. When this happens, it's often Part 2, but at other spots it could be Part 1 or the small-note solo option. The melody line is not reinforced all the time, though, because melody often performs some operation that breaks one of our other guidelines about keeping intervals between the notes as small as we can, avoiding very complicated or quick rhythms, or playing out at the extreme edges of playable ranges. In those spots, we may have opted for whole notes that reinforce a vital note of the chord, for example.

» REINFORCEMENT OF CHOIR HARMONY These band parts are able to stand on their own, anytime the corresponding choir harmony lines are not being sung. But they go well with the choir harmony lines too, even joining up with them in certain moments. These companion volumes afford band directors a wonderful opportunity either to begin or to increase their collaborative efforts with the choir!

» REINFORCEMENT OF TEXTURES IN KEYBOARD It's expected that normally the keyboard arrangement will be played when these pieces are performed. A glance through the Full Scores of the songs will show that we often echoed in the band instrument parts the movements and textures that appear in the piano accompaniment. Each of the parts fits well with what's happening with the keyboard, and not just with the other instrumental parts.

» PARTS 1 & 2 REINFORCING EACH OTHER Much like a unison approach is taken from time to time in the choir volume, Parts 1 and 2 at times join forces in these pieces, depending on what the moment calls for. When the two parts are not in unison together, they're still tracking together rhythmically most of the time. This can help "weekend warriors" or sight-readers of any skill level to keep track of where they are in the piece. They can gain some solidarity from the player sitting next to them, even if that player is reading a different part.

» VOCAL CUES Vocal cues are provided in these arrangements. These cues, the first couple of words to every verse or chorus, can be life savers to volunteer band players, helping them to keep track of where they are while playing the song, especially in those pieces with multiple verses. Vocal cues can be found in the Melody part, Parts 1 and 2, and Bass part.

UNIQUE HARMONY TEXTURES——
Many of these fifteen songs appear in other TMP publications. Here are a few examples of anthologies you may already have in your library, where you'll find cross-publications of piano accompaniment or a lead sheet of our band volume pieces: *Gates of Song* (e.g., "Yism'chu"), the *Ruach* series (e.g., "Oseh Shalom"), the URJ Biennial songbook series (e.g, "L'chah Dodi"), *The Complete Chanukah Songbook* (e.g., "Light One Candle"), *The Complete Shireinu* (e.g., "Y'did Nefesh"), the *Shabbat Anthology* series (e.g., "Ahavat Olam"), *Chazak V'Ematz* (e.g., "Olam Chesed Yibaneh"), *Sing Unto God: The Debbie Friedman Anthology* ("Mi Shebeirach"), *Dan Nichols Anthology* ("Mi Chamochah"), or *Kol B'Seder Anthology* ("Shalom Rav").

A question like this one might arise: assuming I've transposed for the correct key, can I use these "Oseh Shalom" band parts while my accompanying instruments play the chords from the *Ruach* songbook?

The short answer is "no." For many of the songs in this set of volumes, the chord progressions and structure diverge just enough from the versions you'll find in the rest of your Jewish music library that even if you account for key signature, they don't quite cross-pollinate. For example, the chord progressions in this volume for "Ahavat Olam" are not the same as what you'll find in *Shabbat Anthology Volume I.* None of the cross-publications should be leaned on as interchangeable in melody line, structure, setting, or chord progressions with the resources offered in the *Kol Han'shamah* volumes.

VERSATILITY OF USE——
Because it's expected that the keyboard arrangement will be played, players are given melodic or harmonic lines in most intro bars of the song, and these align with the keyboard intro. As a director, you could consider every intro as "optional," depending on what works for your group for a given service or performance. For the most part, this optional introduction is given to the single player of the small-note option line, when available.

In general, our goal was to keep your players playing throughout every piece. There are moments here and there in a song when one or more part lays out, for variety or to give our ears and mouths a break. You'll see recommendations for tacet spots, especially in songs with several verses. But in general, players are given lines from the beginning of the song all the way to the end.

HANDS-ON APPROACHES——
This feature of "maximal playing" means that band directors have maximal flexibility. Directors can and should when possible take a hands-on approach and work with the arrangements as though they're dynamic documents, overlaying onto the parts their own adjustments and guidance, tailored for their particular players and events.

You might decide that in verse 3 of "Adon Olam" you'd like the Part 1 players to play Part 2, and vice versa, for variety. For players who struggle with lower notes or who have somewhat of a "honky" tone in that register, you might invite them to play certain phrases of their part up an octave. You might add an extra crescendo or other dynamic marking to a song, to enrich the delivery, or instruct your players to write in strategic breath marks.

If some of your players are relatively new to their instruments or their embouchures are out of practice and they need to build up more stamina before playing for too long of stretches in one go, then you could build in chops breaks. For example:

In songs with an A section and a B section they could play on the B sections only. In songs with verses they could play on the choruses only. Whatever your preferences may be, you are in good hands with this book! You can get creative.

HANDS-OFF APPROACHES——
Other directors may want to hand out the parts to their players with very little, if any, prior planning. That's okay too—these arrangements are painstakingly designed to set your players up for success, with minimal oversight. If your style is more hands-off, or if you're short on time, then the beauty of this book is that it's plug-and-play. Pass out the sheet music copies, clear your throat, and announce, "Let's take it from the top!"

If you don't have time to strategize about all the ways you could customize these arrangements or the ways you could add your own fingerprints to how the song will be rendered within a service, then you're in the right place, too. That work has largely been done for you during the arranging process.

IN SERVICE TO THE SERVICE——
There's quite a lot going on in each of the fifteen songs, with so many moving pieces: choir, keyboard, guitar, bass, and potentially many band instruments. Not to mention the gathered congregants who may be trying to sing along. While the players have avenues open to them to play during nearly 100 percent of each song, the band is not intended to be the only featured dimension of the whole picture. While the parts were being written, this question was foremost in mind: "What will best serve what's going on in the service?"

The ambition in writing these band lines was to only add to the power and meaning of that particular song, not subtract; and to give support to the song's function in a service, never take away from it. By keeping the reins tight on the arranging, by keeping the lines uncomplicated, and by resisting the urge to crank up the embellishments, we can be better assured that we're not getting in the way of the song's essence and purpose.

A GUIDE TO WORKING WITH YOUR BAND

By Emily Tummons

——YOUR PEOPLE

Your band may have been handed down to you when you stepped in to take over your role from someone else. Or, you may have created or are about to create your whole band from the bottom up. You might be a proficient and experienced band director, interested in fresh tips. Or, maybe you're a leader who's worked with vocalists before, but you're brand new to working with instrumentalists, and you're looking to find your footing. In any case, finding new members and keeping them, working around the edges to cultivate a flourishing and welcoming musical community—that's a challenge for us all! It's a long-term endeavor that can reap an enormous harvest.

In this section we'll explore some ways to seek out newcomers, get them plugged in, encourage them, and help them build their skills. Throughout this section, think in terms of "seasons." In your community, if your players can sign up for one or more rehearsal seasons of the year, and each rehearsal season has a defined start week and stop week (with at least one week "off" before and after the season), then you've got excellent entry points built in for potential new members all year round.

If you have one band and that band plays on semi-regular Friday nights or Saturday mornings continually, think about when throughout the year you could still build in small breaks, so players can be given temporary exit ramps and on-ramps.

RECRUITING AND KEEPING NEW PLAYERS——

» BEYOND BEGINNER The *Kol Han'shamah* band parts are ideal for players from professional to amateur. They were not written with brand-new beginners in mind. When you write up your recruiting materials to place in announcement sheets or newsletters, give some thought to that wording. Invite everyone "from professional to amateur" or "from amateur to professional" to join your ensemble. Players should already know the fingering for their instrument's notes. They should arrive to your band having already learned how to read music (e.g., how to follow roadmaps and dynamics markings) and how to play in tune with others. Once they have mastered those beginning fundamentals, they'll be a great fit for a volunteer synagogue band.

» PUBLICITY The very best time to recruit new members each year might be the High Holy Days (HHD)—not necessarily because the band will be playing for HHD services, but because this is when the highest number of congregants enter our houses of prayer and read the announcement sheets we write for them. This might be one of the moments of the year when you can cast the widest net and raise the highest awareness and visibility of your band across your community.

Consider writing a blurb for your HHD announcement sheet that invites new band players to sign up for one of the seasons in the coming year. Include your contact information, and encourage everyone reading the bulletin to reach out to you if they play an instrument. If you have a rehearsal season already planned for, say, Chanukah (or whichever of your rehearsal seasons immediately follows the HHDs), then list the actual rehearsal dates and times in that blurb. Other spots to consider spreading the word:

- Visit the next board meeting, religious school service, adult education gathering, or choir practice, and ask people to keep the band on their radar and to send folks your way if they play instruments with proficiency.

- Write an article to appear in your congregation's newsletter, Shabbat announcement sheet, website, printed flyers and posters, social media, or any other communication platform.
- Send out individual, personalized invitations through email, phone calls, handwritten cards in the mail, or chatting with people one-on-one.

» ANNUAL OPEN REHEARSAL One idea for attracting new members could be a yearly "open rehearsal." Talk with band members and strongly encourage them to bring friends. Invite every single instrument player in your community, any level, to come sit in on this session, with no expectation of signing up for a season.

Beginners could be invited to this one-off gathering as well! In addition to some training, beginners would also get a taste of what it will be like to play with the rest of the group down the road, once they have mastered the basics. All participants would have the benefits of—in addition to real practice and skill-building—meeting new people, deepening their bonds with those they already know, learning some new music, and having a grand time together. Plan some ice breakers, delicious snacks, and unusually fun warm-ups. Choose a couple of the peppier songs in this volume like "Adon Olam," "L'chah Dodi," "Light One Candle," "Shalom Aleichem," or "Shir Chadash," and dive in.

The right moment of the year for this event will depend on your community's calendar. One possible moment could be in the spring: in the weeks following Passover, but before the High Holy Day rehearsal season for bands or choirs have moved into full swing (and before families start up their summer travels). Or for your community, sometime in January or February might work best. If you already know your next nine to twelve months of schedule and programming on that day, it would be great to have that available to hand out to everyone. Encourage the attendees to look over the rehearsal seasons in the upcoming year, as well as the special events on the horizon when a band will be featured, and to sign up for one or more seasons if they would like to.

» A BAND FOR ALL SEASONS In this guide, we refer to "seasons" throughout the year. A season could be defined as the series of regular rehearsals that build toward a special prayer service or other culminating event when the band will play in public.

Leaders could find it useful to let the ground lie fallow for at least one week in between seasons, even if a "season" in your community refers to something like four months in a row when the band practices every week and plays at synagogue on the third Friday night each month, for example. Allowing for a bit of a reset button on either end comes with a myriad of benefits and almost no downsides.

Some of the advantages of taking a seasonal approach may include time for cleaning out binders and replenishing with new sheet music, a palate-cleansing chance to catch up on and reshuffle other administrative tasks, higher player participation over the scope of the year (an all-or-nothing approach can at times deter players who know they can't commit to every week or even every month), and others.

You could even name each season's band. A very rudimentary approach could look something like this: the Chanukah Band, the Erev Simchat Torah Band, the Kids Choir Band, the Adar Band, the Shabbat Shirah Band, the Bar/Bat Mitzvah Band, the Kislev Band, etc., perhaps including your congregation's name in the titles, too. Naming the band after the season can be an interesting change of pace and can work well for recurring seasons, like above. It works even better for one-off rehearsal seasons, when there's no expectation that the event will come back around again the following year, or at least not with the same musical approach, for example: the Rabbi's Installation Band, the Levin Bat Mitzvah Morning Band, the Building Dedication Band, the First Passover Festival Morning Band, the Baby Naming Band, etc.

It could be that you have a band every single Friday night or every Saturday. If that's the case, you may still want to identify a week here or there during the year when no rehearsals are held and everyone gets at least one week to rest. And it's at those times when you can intentionally bring new members on board in a bundle and get them oriented to joining for the next season, however long or short that stretch of time may be.

An advantage to taking the seasonal approach, whether or not you try out seasonal names as well, is that it gives you, the director, a little more freedom to shift the make-up of your ensembles throughout the year. If there are certain seasons when you need to hand-select more skilled instrumentalists and you don't hold open sign-ups for that group, players' feelings may have less of a chance of getting hurt if this is a shift for a season that has a beginning and an end and if that specialized group was built (in name, in repertoire, and in duration) around a singular event in time and not built around the ongoing core identity of the synagogue.

BUILDING AN INCLUSIVE BAND COMMUNITY——

It's good to get to know every player as well as possible. Pay close attention to their musical strengths and weaknesses, from a technical standpoint. This will help you in matching them up with the right part to play in each song. It will also help you in equipping them to increase their skills over time. Because the context of our volunteer band is a spiritual community, we are able to get to know our players on a more personal level as well and create authentic friendships with them.

Your band brings together players with a wide variety of skills, coming from different walks of life. Your band can demonstrate how we include everyone; the band is a community within a community, where "weekend warriors" serve shoulder to shoulder with the pros. Your band can set an example that we include people who don't have a Jewish background into our circles, playing side by side with our members. Everyone who has breath is invited to make music and to pray.

Many of you have been serving your communities long enough to have a good sense of how to prepare musical guests who have never participated in a Jewish service before. Here are some tips if your group is due for a refresher. The next time that you lead a rehearsal, try to observe with some objectivity any "inside" lingo that comes up. For example:

> "We'll play this song after the *Amidah*."
> "Let's make a walkway around our chairs, for when people go back and forth to the *bimah*."
> "At that point, go ahead and flip over to 'V'zot HaTorah,' and be ready to play it after the last *aliyah*."
> "I'll nod at you all to go back to your seats after *Kaddish*."

The Hebrew terms listed above may or may not come up for your group, but there will be many others that do come up. As you encounter terms that your players may not be familiar with, consider adding these to a continually evolving one-page document that you can share with these players. You can define all the terms your players will need on that sheet.

You might also consider adding a section of broader guidance for players who are new to Jewish prayer spaces. Try to imagine what they might appreciate knowing before participating in their first service. For example: "We try not to let our prayer books touch the floor," or "On Shabbat and holy days, please keep phones and other devices turned off and out of sight," and the like.

——YOUR INSTRUMENTS

In this section, we'll take a quick tour through a representative sampling of common instruments that might drop in to your band in upcoming seasons. As you move through the pages that follow, you may want to flip over to the Instrumental Chart from time to time. That page shows a breakdown, at a glance, of the keys, clefs, relative tuning pitches, and more for some of the instruments you'll likely have in your band. The instruments spotlighted below are divided into the categories we also see in the Instrumental Chart: woodwinds, brass, and strings. Insights are offered on the unique tone qualities (timbre) of each one and advice for which part to give which instrument. As you start mapping out part distribution, keep in mind that the volume of some instruments (e.g., trumpet, oboe, saxophone) may carry better than others in your sanctuary with no amplification. Less forceful instruments (e.g., flute, clarinet, strings) may need the help of a microphone for their volume to carry throughout the hall adequately.

WOODWINDS——
The most common woodwinds to join synagogue bands seem to be clarinet, flute, and sometimes alto saxophone. A few others are described around the edges here, too, to provide a quick point of reference for you as the make-up of your ensemble evolves.

» FLUTE AND RECORDER (KEY OF C) The clear and sweet tone of flutes or recorders may need to be amplified with a microphone, depending on the acoustics of your sanctuary and what other instruments will also be playing. Your flautist could be given any part: Part 1, melody, or the small-note solo option for more skilled players. Part 2 is also possible for flute, although players may find they need to play it an octave higher at times, depending on the song and your ensemble's balance.

Flutes and recorders can be paired with most other instruments within the same part, blending well with other woodwinds, strings, and even some brass instruments. When the word "recorder" is used, this usually refers to the soprano recorder. Like the flute, the recorder reads the treble clef. But unlike the flute, the recorder sounds one octave higher than what's written. Keep that in mind if you should need to decide which part to give to a recorder player. The range of the recorder fits inside the range of a flute. The recorder is lacking the entire lowest octave that a flute can play, as well as some of the highest possible flute pitches too. The other main members of the recorder family are also C instruments.

» OBOE (C) The tone quality of this double reed instrument has a distinctive personality. The oboe can produce at times a haunting or yearning tone and at other times a playful energy. The ideal part to give to your oboists is Part 1. If their skill level is very high and Part 1 can be covered well by another instrument, then your oboists may also really shine on the small-note solo option or melody. Because the tone of the oboe can be so penetrating, it may not be as good a fit as other instruments will be for Part 2.

» CLARINET (B♭) The clarinet is able to sound more mellow, rich, and warm than the oboe and less piercing. It's capable of a wide range of tone and color depending on which area of range it's playing in, the skill of the player, and the style of the piece at hand. Choose one of the songs, and listen to the ensemble (first) track of its rehearsal recordings in order to experience what could be the outcome of asking your clarinetist to play Part 1. It would blend beautifully when playing Part 2 or melody as well. And if your clarinetist is your most skilled player, and if Part 1 will already be managed solidly, you could give him or her the small-note solo option (fourth rehearsal track).

» ALTO AND BARITONE SAXOPHONE (E♭) The most commonly played type of saxophone is the alto sax. If someone arrives at your band with saxophone in hand, it's probably an alto sax. This instrument reads from the music labeled ". . . for E♭ Instruments," which means their music is printed a major sixth (four and a half steps) higher than it sounds when they play it. The sax tone quality can be lively and exciting, even edgy. Alto saxophone players could be given whichever of the parts is the right fit for their skill level. If skill levels are equal across instruments and Part 1 is covered, then Part 2 is a great choice for alto sax.

The baritone saxophone reads the same notes off of the same treble clef that the alto saxophone does. It will just sound an octave lower than the alto sax when played. Because it reads treble clef, technically it can play any of the parts—just keep the low octave in mind when making the plan. Another possible way to use a baritone saxophone is at a service when a bass player is not present.

» SOPRANO AND TENOR SAXOPHONES (B♭) It may be rare that a soprano or tenor saxophone player joins your band. But if they do, know that they'll read from the music labeled ". . . for B♭ Instruments," which means their music is printed one whole step higher than it sounds when they play it. Just like in the twosome above, the tenor saxophone reads the same notes off of the same treble clef that the soprano saxophone does. It will just sound an octave lower than the soprano when played.

BRASS——
To read about instruments like trombone, tuba, and French horn, see the section below called "Special Cases." Here in this section, we'll look only at the instrument that's most likely to show up in your band and that can most easily take on one of the primary parts in this volume: the trumpet.

» TRUMPET (B♭) The trumpet boasts considerable volume compared to some others of the instruments that may find themselves in your band, especially woodwinds and strings. For that reason, along with its robust range and tone, it can make sense to give Part 1 or melody to your trumpet player, depending on the composite of your group. The trumpet is also a good choice for Part 2. When you listen to the ensemble (first) track of its rehearsal recordings, the track that includes all the parts playing (and singing) together, you'll hear how interesting and lovely it can sound in the whole mix to invite a trumpet player to tackle Part 2.

STRINGS——
» VIOLIN (C) The tone of the violin can be soaring, lyrical, with a rich texture. The violin, like the clarinet, so often takes a lead role in Jewish music. You can use the skill level of your violinist and the overall make-up of your band to help you decide which part to give your violinist. Your less-skilled violin players should be given Part 2. Players with more skill can be given any other part. We selected the violin to play the optional small-note solo part in the rehearsal tracks that accompany this volume. Take a moment to listen to the ensemble (first) track of one of the fifteen songs. Notice the effect of a violinist on that higher, optional harmony line, which contains more complexity than Parts 1 and 2.

» VIOLA (C) Viola players primarily read alto clef, and that is not one of the clefs provided in this volume. Most viola players can also read treble clef, however, because printed music makes use of this clef when viola lines move into higher registers. All other things being equal, viola would be a wonderful instrument to play Part 2. It's darker and denser in tone than the crystalline violin and can be relied upon to manage the "middle voices" of an arrangement well, much like the more mellow dimension of clarinet, French horn, and even bassoon. That being said, don't hesitate to ask him or her to play the most prominent harmony line, Part 1, if that person is your most skilled band member.

» CELLO (C) The cello is one of the most versatile instruments, capable of creating a most melancholy tone and a bright and crisp one. If you've got a cellist in your band with at least average skill, you can give the player absolutely any one of these parts with no hesitation: Part 1, played as written or an octave lower; Part 2, played as written; the small-note solo option, played an octave lower; the Melody for Bass Clef Instruments; or the bass line. (If your cellist happens to be the only band instrumentalist at a service, give him or her Part 1, just as you might for any solitary player.) The cellist reads three clefs: bass clef, tenor clef, and treble clef. Tenor clef, like alto clef, is not one that is provided in this volume. So share with the cello player either a C part in treble clef or a C part in bass clef, depending on where you'd like to place this instrument in the overall make-up of your ensemble for that particular service. If you don't have a cello-playing congregant, but your synagogue already has a good working relationship with a cellist who serves in the role of playing the "Kol Nidrei" piece each year during Yom Kippur, consider inviting him or her into a guest spot in your synagogue band from time to time.

» DOUBLE BASS (C) In services when you have double bass players on hand, rather than electric bass guitarists, invite them to use their discretion in switching between *pizzicato* (plucking the strings) and *arco* (bowing the strings) when giving them the bass part. Note that just like with the electric bass, the double bass notes will sound an octave lower than what's printed when played.

SPECIAL CASES——
Here are some notes about instruments with characteristics that are off the beaten path:

» BASS CLEF INSTRUMENTS: BASSOON, TROMBONE, AND TUBA The bassoon, a double-reed woodwind like the oboe, and the trombone and tuba all read bass clef, and all are C instruments. These players have a few different options in your band, depending on what other instruments you may already have with you for a given event. Here are a few choices: play the Melody for Bass Clef Instruments; play the bass line (especially tuba); play Part 2, if the player (especially bassoon or trombone) happens to be able to read treble clef and is able to adjust for the right octave when needed.

A cellist or a baritone saxophone player could also take one of these above options, playing in a very low register. But those two instruments are not included here as special cases, because those players are reliably able to read treble clef.

BAND INSTRUMENTS IN OTHER KEYS——

Music is only provided in this volume for three main zones: for C-instrument treble clef (melody in bass clef, too), for B♭-instrument treble clef, and for E♭-instrument treble clef. We've seen above how the vast majority of band and orchestra instruments fall into these categories.

There are a few instruments that are keyed differently from any of the above registers. Some instruments are in the key of F, like the English horn and the French horn. It may be rare that a player of one of these instruments would like to join your band. Often someone who plays English horn also plays oboe, and someone who plays French horn may also play another brass instrument. If that's the case, invite the player to play one of these alternative instruments, so that he or she can jump into the mix right away, with no need to transpose a part.

——YOUR MATERIALS

COMPILING BINDERS——

This section walks through some of the ins and outs of assembling everyone's binder. At rehearsal, in a given player's binder you might find items like these: a page of warm-up exercises, the rehearsal season schedule, a half-page rehearsal agenda for that session, sheet music, copies of siddur pages or readings in the service you're preparing for, and a cue sheet from the prior service that serves as a table of contents during rehearsals.

If you're distributing your purchased digital part files to players who request a digital rather than physical copy, consider organizing your file system into folders by instrument or by player. That way, you can simply send a link to that folder to a particular player without overwhelming them with other parts to choose from. For physical copies, it is convenient to three-hole punch these items for the players' binders on both the left edge and the right edge. Many of you are already in this habit—if not, consider starting it up. Printing on only one side and hole-punching on both sides gives you more options when it's time to assemble the binders. It gives the players more options too. The player may decide to flip around some of the orientations depending on difficulty levels of various page turns. Hole-punching both sides can make everybody's life easier.

» SHEET MUSIC When preparing the music, you might annotate along the top of the printouts which instrument that part is for, the name of the person playing it, and which of the parts on the page you want them to play if there's more than one on the page. Here's a sample rundown for one song:

# of copies:	Which Part:	Instrument:	Name:	What to Play:
1	Full Score	band director	Emily	
3	PVG	keyboard	Nanette	
		lead vocalist	Cantor	
		other vocalist	Judith	
2	Lead Sheet / Melody for C Inst.	guitar	Emily	
		percussion	Larry M.	
1	Bass	electric bass	Randy	
1	Melody for Bass Clef Inst.	cello	Larry F.	melody
2	Parts 1 and 2 for C Inst.	violin	Carmen	small-note option
		flute	Betsy	Part 1
1	Parts 1 and 2 for B♭ Inst.	clarinet	Warren	Part 1
1	Parts 1 and 2 for E♭ Inst.	alto saxophone	Ron	Part 2

In the list above, we can see that the violinist and flautist are reading from the same music even though they were given individual copies. The benefit of having all three parts (Part 1, Part 2, and the small-note solo option) printed together on the same sheet music is that if you needed to ask the violin and flute to switch the parts they're playing, mid-rehearsal, you don't need to run and print out new sheet music for them; they will just read a different line on the page. Use that to your advantage when experimenting with balance and overall sound texture during the early rehearsals of each season.

In a very large orchestra or band, whether student or professional, there's a lot of sharing of music stands and sharing of sheet music. If there were a music stand in front of every single player, it would be hard to make those concentric, arced rows be very curved. Those orchestras can share music stands and sheet music because there is high reliability that all players will attend each rehearsal and show up for the culminating concert.

In volunteer synagogue bands, we may not have the luxury of knowing with certainty that all instrumentalists who have signed up for a season will be able to actually attend every rehearsal and service. Keep that in mind when setting up music stands and planning for when music might be shared during a rehearsal or service, versus when the players read from their own individual sheet music. Either way, know that the size of the noteheads for Parts 1 and 2 has been intentionally printed larger than, for example, the PVG part, so that sharing music is easy when needed.

» INTERSPERSING READINGS Unless the players have two separate music stands, they will likely not be grappling with both a siddur and a sheet-music-filled binder. When volunteers try to handle both on a music stand, one book usually falls off, and it's usually the prayer book. It is a really nice touch, if you're able and have the appropriate licensing and permission from the publisher, to include a few key English readings in your players' binders, if you know that they will be at their stations for those segments and they won't have prayer books handy. This could include the Hebrew characters and transliteration for Mourner's *Kaddish*. (If the format is digital, consider adding them to a master file containing sheet music and service pages.) Imagine the flow of the service from the perspective of this player at this station, and ask yourself, "How can I help this person feel more engaged and connected throughout the service, even when they're not playing?"

—MAKING GREAT CUE SHEETS

The printed order of the service, or a "cue sheet" as some communities refer to it, doesn't just include a list of songs and readings. The cue sheet can rope in other core details and logistical prompts that can make a world of difference in how smoothly that service flows.

For a service, there are so many folks who might need a cue sheet: the sound engineer, cantor, rabbi, lay leaders, singers, or players. When it's time to provide copies, write each person's name at the top of the sheet, and place it on their music stand or in their hands before sound check begins. For rehearsals, if the cue sheet for the service you're practicing toward is not yet finalized, then a cue sheet from a similar past service can serve as a great table of contents for the binder or digital file, helping the player flip to that song quickly. This frees you up, as the director, to move through songs in whatever order you want—you don't have to go in the order the songs appear in the binder just to make practice more efficient. Another benefit to making sure your rehearsal binders or files include a cue sheet is that players need to get accustomed to reading your particular flavor and format of cue sheet over time, before encountering one at the service where they're playing.

SITTING, STANDING, RELOCATING——

When during the service, if ever, would you like your band players to stand? When might they start standing up if they're on auto pilot, but you'd rather them not?

For example, if you would like your instrument players to stay seated during their playing of the last verse of "L'chah Dodi," then you can specify that in the cue sheet. If you'd like for the whole band to stand while playing the last verse of "L'chah Dodi," you should practice these movements during rehearsals, in addition to layering these cues into the cue sheet.

The decision of whether to sit or stand during this or that liturgical piece deserves at least passing attention when it comes to vocalists. For band players, it is another animal entirely. Many players cannot physically play their instruments while standing. For others, if they will be called upon to stand for some songs and not others, then they may need to stand for most songs because going back and forth quickly from song to song may not be possible for them.

Give some thought as well to what you would like your players to do while they are not playing. Will your players be at their band stations (but not playing) around the segments of *Bar'chu*, the *Amidah*, *Aleinu*, or the Mourner's *Kaddish*? If so, make a judgment call on whether or not they should be invited to stand during these prayers. If you want to go for it, be sure to give them clear instructions on what to keep in mind when standing (e.g., taking care not to knock over instruments, cups with reeds soaking, music stands, instrument microphones). If facing the ark is part of your music team's practice during certain sections of the service, then you might give some thought to how to instruct your players in this regard too.

If prayer choreography is expected of band players, be sure to orient your players who are new to Jewish services. They are in a visually exposed spot—helping to prepare them is another way to show them hospitality and make them feel at ease. If there will be a very wide swath of time when the band is not playing, take time to strategize how to handle that. Weigh the pros and cons of asking the band to stay put, versus giving them cues for going to the pews for a while and then returning to their stations to play another song. A choir filing out of a choir loft can be very orderly and even fast (and this is often rehearsed). A band may have many more logistical challenges to contend with. Either way, it's a good idea to layer any instructions into the cue sheet and to practice all movements (and unexpected non-movements) at rehearsals.

WHAT'S NEXT?——

It's great to place something at the very end of every cue sheet, after the postlude, that reminds musicians of whatever you would like them to do right after the service. This spot could also remind them of the next event coming up, to keep on their radar. Here are some examples:

- "Please place this cue sheet in the front pocket of your binder—we'll use it as a table of contents for our next rehearsal."
- "Choir singers: please place your binders on the cart at the back of the sanctuary after the service. Band players: please leave your binders on your chairs. Shabbat shalom!"
- "Immediately after the service, please come help our clergy team lead *Kiddush* and *Motzi*, and we'll put away our instruments and binders after that."
- "Music-makers: have a great Shabbat, and we'll see you at rehearsal next Wednesday, 7 p.m."

OTHER SUPPLIES——
Carrying stacks of binders out each week from their storage spot over to the rehearsal station can be back breaking. The one single supply or piece of equipment that's made the biggest difference for me in setting up and running band and choir rehearsals has been the wheeled mail cart. If you have a lot of musicians and can afford to buy two of them, use one for choir binders and one for band binders. In the top half of the cart can be kept all the band members' binders for that rehearsal season (binders for other seasons can be stored in normal non-mobile shelving). Then there's only one sweeping motion when preparing for a rehearsal or a service: pushing the wheeled cart from the room where it sits over to a spot where the players can easily grab their own binder when they arrive, placing it back in the cart after the rehearsal.

In the bottom half of the cart can be kept all the supplies and other odds and ends needed for rehearsals. Here are some supplies that could be nice to have nearby for your season: paper clips, a three-hole punch, pencils, a pencil sharpener, highlighters, empty binders for walk-ins, accordion files with extra copies of sheet music, dry-erase markers and eraser, gaffer tape, extra copies of the rehearsal dates or upcoming events for the band, and perhaps a label maker, extra electronic tuner, or extra music stand light.

——YOUR REHEARSALS

Every rehearsal carries a cost. It may be the cost of salaried staff members' time, the hourly or per rehearsal cost of the paid professionals, the cost of time and energy from our lay volunteers, or simply the cost of cooling, heating, electricity, water, and custodial time. However high or low our per-rehearsal costs might be, it pays to plan each one well and run it with agility.

Each rehearsal also carries value! Your band players make friends, bond with each other, laugh together, and pray together. They also grow in their musicality with each passing season, sharpening their technique, developing their skills with rhythm, expression, listening, and blending. Each rehearsal has the potential to add qualitative and quantitative worth to the lives of all the participants. Here are a few collected tips and insights that can help maximize value in your band's next rehearsal season:

PLANNING FOR A GREAT REHEARSAL——
» SCHEDULING When singers arrive late to choir practice, it can be disruptive and cuts into the amount of time the group can work productively that session. When band players arrive late, it is compounded much more, because their equipment requires more set-up than that of singers. Here is a tip for curbing late arrivals in your volunteer band:

Visually, if you can list all of your rehearsals as having an optional start time earlier than the actual start time, you may dramatically improve punctuality. Let's say an upcoming rehearsal season spans five weeks of Wednesday evenings. The way it is printed in flyers and email reminders could look something like this:

Chanukah Band Rehearsals
Wednesdays, 7:00 p.m.–8:30 p.m. (optional warm-up and social time: 6:45 p.m.)

By explicitly planning for all of your rehearsals to have a "soft opening" fifteen minutes before the start time, you're acknowledging that socializing is actually one of the legitimate goals for your group, and you're carving out time to make it intentional. You are also acknowledging that your band members have practical needs that your choir members do not have. Band members have a lot of equipment. They need extra time to assemble their instrument, go store their cases somewhere where they won't be tripped over, perhaps soak reeds, and begin to blow the dust out of the instrument before the group warm-ups begin. Listing your times this way gives assurance to your players that the doors of the building and the rehearsal room will be open early, the lights will be on, the heating or cooling system will treat 6:45 p.m. as the start time and not 7:00 p.m., and if they want to catch up with a friend before practice, your practice environment is set up for them to do that. A few of your players may do this anyway, showing up ten minutes early to a rehearsal without needing a plainly marked announcement that it is okay to arrive early. And at the stroke of 7:00 p.m. they're in place and ready to play the group's first note. Many won't, though; and making this early, optional time segment official can absorb a lot of logistical needs that arise. Volunteers do better if there is a window of time they should shoot for in their arrival, and not just one singular moment of arrival to aim for. If they are not given a visually printed window prior to the start time, many inadvertently treat the first fifteen minutes of practice as their window of arrival time to aim for (in this case, 7:00–7:15 p.m.).

» SETTING GOALS Depending on the size of your band, you might find it useful to make the first rehearsal week of every season targeted only at accompanying instruments: piano, guitars, bass, and percussion. These are the core players of your band. Consider bringing them in first, in order to lay the groundwork and establish the grooves of the songs. Then start adding the band instrument players in the following week or two.

If you have time, make a rehearsal agenda for each practice, no matter if it's the broad group or a sub-group. The agenda could be written out on a large dry-erase board or printed and placed on the players' stands before practice begins. This list could include the order that you'll move through everything and a few bullet points of goals for each piece or exercise. Sharing the order and the aims with the group helps reinforce the purpose of the practice and increases the chances that the goals can be accomplished. Announcements and reminders can be printed on this whiteboard or handout, too.

» INVITING IN YOUR CLERGY PARTNERS In your rehearsals, who among the clergy team is not typically present? Consider inviting her or him for a visit at least once per rehearsal season. For some synagogue bands, the cantor is the band director, so the rabbi could be invited in for a visit. In volunteer bands where neither the cantor nor the rabbi is the band director, both could be invited to bring greetings.

Here are just a few examples of the many good outcomes of a visit by a clergy partner: a pragmatic walk-through of cues for the upcoming service, noting how the clergy role in the service interacts with the band's role; a moment of inspiration and insight, reminders of the shared purpose of the group or the service; an opportunity for the clergy to get to know your band players better and for them to get to know the clergy better; a chance for the players to be thanked sincerely by the spiritual leader of the congregation for all of their hard work that season; your chance as band director to get feedback from the clergy on the sound of the songs or the acoustics in the sanctuary; a chance for the clergy to teach the players something about the Hebrew lyrics or liturgical context of one of your pieces; and so on.

——RUNNING A GREAT REHEARSAL

» KICK THINGS OFF WITH A SONG It is so nice to start things off with a song, right at the stroke of "start time." It rewards every player who arrived early and is ready to begin on time. It can set a bright and positive mood for the practice that follows. It feels more like the rehearsal is officially underway, more so than beginning with announcements, tuning, or warm-ups.

In band rehearsals, this is not commonly done—groups don't tend to start off with a song. There are a lot of good reasons for this. If the song you're using to kick off your practice is one of your core rehearsal pieces, then it can actually be counterproductive. Some players are still arriving and will miss out on critical guidance and practice for that piece, no one is in tune yet with the rest of the players, latecomers may have missed the mention of which page you're on or where to find the piece in the binder, and bad habits and outcomes can flow from diving right into a challenging piece, cold, with instruments and embouchures that are not warmed up properly.

That's why, for band practice, it can be useful and even fun to go a different route. Start the rehearsal instead with the singing of your community's go-to setting of "Hineih Mah Tov." The words can be printed in everyone's binder, with no copies of music notation needed. The beauty of this is that instrumentally the only player who needs to be in tune and ready for prime time the moment the rehearsal begins is one single accompanying instrument, like your guitarist or pianist. Provide the sheet music to that player.

Everyone else simply sings. They sing if they're already seated in their stations and ready to go. They sing if they're still walking in the door or still quickly assembling their instruments off to the side.

Not all band players consider themselves "singers" (and this opening song should not include a goal of striving for vocal excellence), but all players will benefit from occasional singing. Singing helps instrumentalists get the notes internalized in a different way from playing. The resonance and intonation when singing feel different from when playing. The impact on ensemble cohesion is different, too. This singing of the same song every week of a particular rehearsal season can have so many benefits: it's a gathering call for stragglers and absorbs latecomers well; it has a centering effect on the group, both musically and spiritually; it's a technique for accomplishing something technically productive right off the bat without latecomers missing something vital in the announcements, for example; and finally, you are all expressing in the text something that everyone genuinely feels: It is so good and beautiful that we can all sit here together right now. After the singing of "Hineih Mah Tov," or whichever gathering song you choose for that rehearsal season, other segments, like warm-ups, announcements, tuning, etc., can begin.

» TUNING In many of the environments where this resource will be used, there will be a keyboard player. The pianist is the one, more than most other players, with the most fixed tuning. He or she carries the immovable pitch, so it's a good idea to have the rest of the players tune to this instrument, rather than to an electric tuner or a wind instrument, for example.

In the Instrumental Chart, directors will find a column showing what note to ask players to play, in order to match concert pitches. Whether you have your band tune to a B♭, an A, or a C, check the chart when you need a quick glance at transpositions for various instruments. For example, to have everyone tune to a concert A pitch, played by the keyboardist, ask the clarinets to play their B; ask the alto saxophones to play their F#. If your keyboardist is experienced with the process of helping various instruments to tune, you could ask him or her to lead that segment of your rehearsal, from the piano.

Or, some of your bands may have a member who used to work as a band director or used to have some leadership role in days gone by. If so, then whether your approach is more hands-on band directing or hands-off band directing, you might still consider delegating to that person the job of managing the tuning moments or warm-up moments in your band rehearsals. If you delegate tuning, give that person a copy of the Instrumental Chart.

Every now and then, during your rehearsal, pause to retune. Help players notice that the small improvements they make in tone quality, support, and balance while playing can impact their intonation every bit as much as having the mouthpiece in exactly the "right" spot.

» WARMING UP Every director has his or her own preferred way of tuning and getting the band players warmed up. You might like something as simple as a B♭ major scale in ascending and descending half notes, printed in the correctly transposed keys for your instrumentalists. Or you might have your own packet of exercises that target rhythm, listening and blending, articulation, dynamics, posture, particular intervals, breathing, ear training, intonation, and more.

Feel free to experiment from one rehearsal season to the next, availing yourself of the many free resources available online. When you need a change of pace, try one of these:

- Play a familiar scale, in unison, with the lights turned off, to focus on keener listening.
- Have players breathe in through the nose for four counts and out for six counts, on repeat, focused on the diaphragm.
- Play a familiar scale in unison, then hum the same scale together. Then, sing it together on a tall "ah" vowel. Now play it again in unison, focused on intonation. What improvements are noticeable?
- As the group plays an ascending scale, ask them to imagine themselves physically moving downward (to help avoid accidentally getting a bit sharper with each note). As they play a descending scale, ask them to imagine themselves physically moving upward (to help them avoid accidentally

getting a bit flatter with each note). You can move your arms in these directions too, to make the mental imaging more vivid and impactful.

Notice which exercises tend to be the most useful and effective for your players, depending on their skill levels and needs. A warm-up segment can not only get their horns and embouchures ready for the task at hand; it can also be a great opportunity to provide to them valuable training in the fundamentals of good technique and musicality. Keep adding to your collection!

» A SHARED PURPOSE Before or after the warm-up segment could be a good time to include an ice-breaker or an interactive moment. The topic could be something as innocuous as "Turn to a player near you: share the name of a favorite '80s movie, and what you like about it."

Or, you could leverage these moments to foster deeper relationships among your teammates. For one of these moments, invite your players to share with one another: "What have you been up to for the last three hours or so?" The answers will be diverse; some may have been buried in work stress, swimming at the gym, feeding their kids, reading a book, walking their dogs, driving through rush hour to get to synagogue, or taking a nap. Some may have been practicing their instrument! The point is that everyone is arriving to this rehearsal in a different mental state, and now it's time to collect ourselves toward a shared purpose.

There may not be time to present full *d'var Torah* segments at each rehearsal, but many band directors find success in offering up some small, centering morsel of insight or encouragement from that week's *parashah*—perhaps a quote by a great Jewish thinker, one that's particularly relevant to that season of the Jewish calendar; perhaps one line from that week's haftarah that's relevant to the evening's music or the event you're preparing for. Whatever you feel compelled to share, or whatever you invite a player to share, taking a moment of shared meaning and humanity can have a grounding and inspiring effect on the group.

» TIPS FOR TACKLING A PIECE The first time you introduce a piece to your band, it could be helpful to have a few extra copies of the Melody for C Instruments part handy. Distribute a few to share among the band, and introduce the piece by singing it.

The rehearsal tracks provided with this volume can be shared with all of your players. They are essential tools for players' individual practice sessions at home. You can also use these rehearsal tracks, to great effect, in the context of a rehearsal. Play the first track of whatever song you're introducing; this track includes every part playing and singing together. Invite players to sing along with the song, not as though they're in a choir, but as though they're in the congregation. They can follow along with the melody part. Ask them to internalize the groove and feel of the song as they sing through it along with the track.

Play it again, this time reading from the Parts 1 and 2 page. Invite your players of Parts 1 and 2 and the optional small-note solo line to ask themselves during that next run-through of the song: Where am I reinforcing the melody line? Encourage them to circle these measures in pencil. These provide anchoring points for the player. They are also important to the overall balance of the song. Players could also notice when their lines are mirrored in the keyboard or the small-note solo option. Experiment with using the second or third part tracks in rehearsal too, and find what's most effective.

The "Three Little Words" method is another that might work for your band. Over the course of the rehearsal season, invite each player to come up with three words to eventually scrawl along the top of their sheet music for a song. These three words are the touchpoints of the song, in the mind of that player, the chief characteristics of the song, the most salient qualities.

As the director, you can look through the piece ahead of time and identify a couple of spots that you think your players might fumble if they're ever playing the song on autopilot. Make your band aware of those spots at rehearsal, and ask everyone to make a pencil or highlighter marking there.

Consider splitting the group up into sections for a segment of the rehearsal. For your band, it could be useful at some rehearsals to have the rhythm section (the full accompanying group possibly including piano, guitar, drums, and bass) branch off from the band instrument players who are reading from Parts 1 and 2 or melody. Then bring the two groups back together.

» BUILDING IN BREAKS Band members who don't play often may not be able to play straight through the length of an entire rehearsal with no playing breaks. It's a great idea to brainstorm what you could place in the midway point of your practice session that is still productive but doesn't involve playing—for example: a visit from clergy or other leaders bringing greetings; announcements; a pause to walk through logistics like when and how going back and forth to the pews may happen in an upcoming service; ice-breaker questions or other guided activities to help your members interact with and get to know one another better; singing "Happy Birthday" to anyone who has had a birthday recently; or even taking of a full break for getting water or going to the restroom.

——YOUR SERVICES

GREAT TIMES OF THE YEAR TO USE YOUR BANDS——

If you are just starting out, think about selecting for your first couple of services a moment of the year that is on the less formal side and preparing only one song: "Adon Olam," to close the service. You could talk with your religious school director to see if your new band could play that song at the children's Sunday morning *t'filah*. Or, talk with the rabbi to find out if your new band could be paired with an outdoor or casual service—perhaps in the summer or one of the evenings of Sukkot. Your new band could play "Adon Olam" to close a service in the month of Adar—perhaps on Erev Purim. Anytime you do this, close a service with "Adon Olam," and get more bang for your buck by playing it again, right after the service, as a postlude.

Allowing your band a debut at an event that is not on par with the High Holy Days or other more solemn and elevated services will help your players get acclimated to participating in community events. And it will give you, their director, a chance to troubleshoot and experiment before taking things up a notch.

Once your band is established, most of the logistical bugs are worked out, and you've got a reliable cast of characters, you can look at just about any time of year as a great chance to invite your band to participate. Plan for your band to play on Shabbat Chanukah or another service surrounding the festival of Chanukah with the inclusion of "Light One Candle" from this volume or "Maoz Tzur" from volume I. Plan an annual outdoor concert near Shavuot or during another summer month. Tie your band to certain festivals, bar and bat mitzvah services—any sacred moment in the life of the congregation. Think about creating a monthly, bi-monthly, or quarterly service that features your band. The sky's the limit.

GOOD SPOTS DURING A SERVICE TO USE YOUR BANDS——

» PRELUDES AND POSTLUDES Playing prelude music in the 5–10 minutes or so leading up to the start of a service can be such a good way to set the tone. If there will be a new song in the service, then this is an opportune time to let congregants gain some familiarity with it, even passively, before it's sung. A prelude fills the space with a spirit of welcome as congregants arrive and get settled. Playing a prelude piece is a boon for the band in another way too: it helps them "break the seal" of playing in the service before it has formally begun. They get to establish their presence while the congregation's attention is only half-focused on them. This can help calm nerves and smoothly transition the players into a functional role of leadership once the service starts.

Let's say the doors of the sanctuary open around 6:00 p.m., and the service begins with the first song at 6:30 p.m. Here's a sample timeline that could work for a band, adapting it for your needs:

5:15 p.m.	Players arriving, settling in, and tuning
5:30 p.m.	Rehearsal begins

6:10 p.m. Rehearsal ends, and bio-break begins
6:20 p.m. Return to station, group photo, and double-check tuning
6:25 p.m. Begin full-band prelude song, segueing into only accompanying instrument(s)
6:30 p.m. Accompanying instrument concludes, and service begins

After the prelude song ends, there will be a small stretch of time, of unpredictable length, leading up to the stroke of 6:30. Consider inviting your pianist or guitarist to take the reins alone for this last bit, and nod when it's time for them to draw their final prelude playing to a close.

Postludes can serve purposes that are a bit different from preludes. A postlude could be any song your band played during the service, perhaps "Shir Chadash" or "Adon Olam" that was just sung at the end, or a different piece. Choose something that will send the congregants on their way with an echo of that service's message or feeling.

The most important thing to keep in mind when planning to play one of these pieces as an instrumental, rather than as a sung piece, is the melody. The melody line becomes the most vital component for a prelude or postlude, so consider giving it to your best player.

» OPENING AND CLOSING SONGS By sticking around after the prelude just long enough to play the opening song of the service and then coming back up early before the postlude to play the closing song, your band has more than doubled its participation level. It's done this by more than doubling its roles in (and just outside) the service, without needing to double the number of pieces it prepares.

If you are just starting out, think along the lines of opening and closing songs, without the pressure to keep your band playing throughout the service just yet. This can be a terrific way to break the ice. Once you have the opening and closing songs down pat, and with a couple of services under your belt, begin branching out into other parts of the service.

» AFTER-SERMON ANTHEM The after-sermon spot of a service can be, especially in Reform services, an opportunity for special music to be shared. This special music often carries with it the intention that the congregation receive the music and its message, and not necessarily that they sing along. When planned out purposefully, the "anthem" has the potential to gather up the insights and meaning conveyed during the sermon and place a seal on it, to allow those insights to now go straight to our hearts if they have not already.

As you and your clergy partners envision the arc of your service, if you find that it will be okay to have your band players staying in place in their stations during the sermon, ready to play right after it, then consider selecting one of the pieces in this volume (one that is evocative of that service's sermon or message). Whether sung by a soloist or a choir singing from the companion volume, a song in this spot of the service can really shine, made all the better by the addition of your band players. Whether or not an anthem is familiar to the congregation, it can be a good candidate for including as a prelude or postlude.

» A SAMPLE PLAN Below is an example of an Erev Shabbat service and how you could engage your band to a moderate degree: not strictly one song and not every song. This sample plan also plots songs out in fairly even distribution over the course of the service. Every time the players come up to their stations, they play at least two pieces before leaving again. This list doesn't include cues or all the other details that would be included on a cue sheet. It is simply a very condensed snapshot of the songs a band could play, in the order they could play them, with important notes about when to relocate:

[Prelude: "Y'did Nefesh," "Shalom Aleichem"]
"Y'did Nefesh," "L'chah Dodi," "Shalom Aleichem" *[then to pews]*
[back up to stations when rabbi begins introducing segment about healing]
"Mi Shebeirach" *[stay in stations during sermon]*
"Olam Chesed Yibaneh" for after-sermon anthem *[then to pews]*

[back to stations during announcements]
"Adon Olam" for closing song
*[Postlude: **"Adon Olam"** and **"Shalom Aleichem"**]*

» STRATEGIC SOUND CHECKS You likely already have a go-to, adaptable checklist that you use for sound checks before services. Here are some more ideas to weave into the mix, if you don't do these already:

- Consider printing a brief list at the top of that service's cue sheet that lists the key items that will be targeted during sound check. That way everyone involved can keep up and follow along well.
- Check the loudest sections of the loudest songs. Check key spots where a certain player may have exposed lines and want to run through them.
- Add to your lists moments from your players' songs that intersect with other participants (like clergy or readers) who may not have been able to attend the regular rehearsal but who need to work out the final bugs in sync with the band, before it takes place in the service.
- Add a note to yourself to check in the moment: is your sound check being broadcast right now? Make sure that whoever may be running your technology knows to give you a heads-up before doing a live-stream test or starting the cameras rolling, if it is not yet the start time of the service. Because there won't be guarantees, it's a good idea to assume that every note that is being played in the sanctuary and everything that is said out loud can be picked up by microphones and accidentally shared with people.
- Take a moment at some point during the sound check to ask everyone: How are your sight lines? Can you see me giving you cues? Can you see the other players or singers whom you need to see? How is the lighting; does anyone need a music stand light? Make adjustments to the monitors or to the way the players are seated so that everyone can hear what they need to hear, and see what they need to see.
- Check walkways. If players need to go to the pews partway through the service and then return to their stations for more playing later, do all of the walkways allow for this? If any of the players uses a walker or a cane, consider adding more gaffer tape to the cables and wires on the floor than normal. Also, if congregants need to pass through the band area, make sure there is a safe path for them.
- If things are going smoothly and the group is not too rushed, some band directors find that this moment, the sound check and rehearsal before a service, can be the best time to grab a group photo. There's more time to take a photo at regular weekly or seasonal rehearsals. But at the sound check before a service, players are more likely to look and feel their best, and attendance is maximal. In the context of a Friday night service, beforehand tends to be a better option than afterward, especially if by the time the service ends Shabbat will have already begun.
- If there's time, run the introductions and final measures of every song the band plays.

——CLOSING THOUGHTS

BEYOND THIS SONGBOOK——

Kol Han'shamah: Band Volume II has given you fifteen new arrangements to begin exploring with your band. In addition, you may already own *Kol Han'shamah: Band Volume I* (TMP), *T'filah Band* (Tara Publications), or *K'lei Zemer* (TMP), which together offer your group many more arrangements. If you haven't already, you might take a few minutes to read the introduction of the companion volume, *Kol Han'shamah: Choir Volume II*. This introduction, written by Cantor Janice Roger, includes many insights and tips that are helpful not only for choir directors but also for band directors.

DEBRIEFING AND EVALUATIONS——

At least once per year, think about distributing a survey widely, to every player who has participated in one or more seasons. The feedback players give in their evaluations can be very illuminating for leaders! Here are some topics to consider inviting your players to weigh in on:

- Day of the week and time of day for typical rehearsals
- Frequency of "performances" throughout the year
- Supplies or materials to gather or purchase that could improve their experience
- Given a list of all other groups and projects of the music program (other choirs, ensembles, programs) where the player is also invited to plug in, and ask which, if any, they'd be interested in learning more about
- Favorite piece from the last year
- Overall ease or difficulty of typical band pieces

Build in time for yourself after the window for filling out the survey has closed to fully take in the results and brainstorm improvements. Follow up one-on-one with players who have asked questions or expressed needs or interest in learning more about something. Talk with your leadership team about what changes to make in the coming year, based on all the feedback you received.

Some band directors find it useful to create a separate survey for congregants. This could go out to half a dozen or more carefully selected synagogue members who are frequent attendees. Ask them questions about the impact the band is having on their experience of synagogue life and worship. From logistical questions about how the sound is carrying to their pew, to broader questions about the energy the band is adding to the culture and *kavanah* of the community, these congregational surveys can be illuminating for you as well.

BEYOND REHEARSAL SEASONS——

» WORKSHOPS Although regular practice on one's own or in private lessons can make all the difference in the world to your ensemble's sound, most of your volunteers may not be able to dedicate themselves to weekly private lessons and practice at home. "Weekend warriors" may be interested in improving their skills, but they may not know how.

Workshops can be a really effective way to inspire your synagogue band to begin practicing in earnest and cultivate their skills. This can also be a good recruiting tool to attract more members. Think about bringing in some area band teachers or people you know who have expertise in the instruments represented in your group or who are great at coaching an ensemble toward creating a cohesive sound. Partnering with another local synagogue band or even a volunteer church band could be a possibility. Hold a collective workshop, with training that members of both bands will find enriching. If the two groups seem to gel, think about planning an event together, whether a community concert or interfaith service.

» CELEBRATION EVENTS If you don't already hold an event each year that celebrates the players in your band, consider trying it out! Throw them a party, even if it is very low-budget, like a simple gathering at a park. Encourage the players to help you organize things and to invite their families to come with them. Getting together for an annual shebang gives players a chance to bond and celebrate with each other, and it gives leaders a chance to build excitement about the year to come and say thanks for all the hard work of the past year.

From one year to the next, you may have one or more players you'd like to give official recognition to, either at a celebratory event with the band or at, for example, a "Volunteer Shabbat" service. The CCAR (Central Conference of American Rabbis) offers several options of beautiful certificates that can help make formal your heartfelt appreciation for them.

EVERYTHING THAT BREATHES——

This songbook seeks to be a useful tool for you as you build inclusive and joyful synagogue bands. There's really no right or wrong technique to bring that to fruition. More than the notes on the page, it's the passion, wisdom, and skill that you bring to your directing work that help your band to flourish. Every time you tell one of your players, "You belong here—you're one of us," or "You are a gift to our community," you're spreading out a shelter of belonging over them. Through your hard work and thoughtful leadership, you're building the sort of band where *kol han'shamah* ("everything that breathes," Psalm 150) is invited to join in. Every breathing soul can find its voice. And all those voices can be gathered together, toward elevating the prayers of your congregation, toward infusing your house of worship with energy and joy.

May your work continue to be rewarding, fruitful, and fun. Good luck in your next season, and may you go from strength to strength!

TRACK LIST FOR ACCOMPANYING ALBUM

Arrangements by Emily Tummons

ADON OLAM
Traditional
1. Master Track with voices and instruments
2. Part 1 Practice Track
3. Part 2 Practice Track
4. Small-Note Solo Instrument Practice Track

AHAVAT OLAM
Eric Mandell
5. Master Track with voices and instruments
6. Part 1 Practice Track
7. Part 2 Practice Track
8. Small-Note Solo Instrument Practice Track

BAR'CHU
Rachelle Nelson
9. Master Track with voices and instruments
10. Part 1 Practice Track
11. Part 2 Practice Track
12. Small-Note Solo Instrument Practice Track

L'CHAH DODI
Aaron Bensoussan
13. Master Track with voices and instruments
14. Part 1 Practice Track
15. Part 2 Practice Track
16. Small-Note Solo Instrument Practice Track

LIGHT ONE CANDLE
Peter Yarrow
17. Master Track with voices and instruments
18. Part 1 Practice Track
19. Part 2 Practice Track
20. Small-Note Solo Instrument Practice Track

MI CHAMOCHAH
Dan Nichols and Mason Cooper
21. Master Track with voices and instruments
22. Part 1 Practice Track
23. Part 2 Practice Track
24. Small-Note Solo Instrument Practice Track

MI SHEBEIRACH
Debbie Friedman
25. Master Track with voices and instruments
26. Part 1 Practice Track
27. Part 2 Practice Track
28. Small-Note Solo Instrument Practice Track

OLAM CHESED YIBANEH
Menachem Creditor
29. Master Track with voices and instruments
30. Part 1 Practice Track
31. Part 2 Practice Track
32. Small-Note Solo Instrument Practice Track

OSEH SHALOM
Elana Jagoda
33. Master Track with voices and instruments
34. Part 1 Practice Track
35. Part 2 Practice Track
36. Small-Note Solo Instrument Practice Track

SHALOM ALEICHEM
Sol Zim
37. Master Track with voices and instruments
38. Part 1 Practice Track
39. Part 2 Practice Track
40. Small-Note Solo Instrument Practice Track

SHALOM RAV
Jeff Klepper and Dan Freelander
41. Master Track with voices and instruments
42. Part 1 Practice Track
43. Part 2 Practice Track
44. Small-Note Solo Instrument Practice Track

SHIR CHADASH
Julie Silver
45. Master Track with voices and instruments
46. Part 1 Practice Track
47. Part 2 Practice Track
48. Small-Note Solo Instrument Practice Track

Y'DID NEFESH
Ehud and Sarah Zweig
49. Master Track with voices and instruments
50. Part 1 Practice Track
51. Part 2 Practice Track
52. Small-Note Solo Instrument Practice Track

YIH'YU L'RATZON
Hollis Schachner
53. Master Track with voices and instruments
54. Part 1 Practice Track
55. Part 2 Practice Track
56. Small-Note Solo Instrument Practice Track

YISM'CHU
Traditional Chasidic
57. Master Track with voices and instruments
58. Part 1 Practice Track
59. Part 2 Practice Track
60. Small-Note Solo Instrument Practice Track

Vocals: **Cantor Emma Lutz** and **Cantor Billy Tiep**; Piano: **Tali Tadmor**. Small-Note Solo Instrument (violin): **Rebecca Beerstein**; Part 1 (clarinet): **Jacob Freiman**; Part 2 (trumpet): **Remy Ohara**; Bass: **Skyler Lee**.

Produced by Joel Eglash; engineered by Laura Agudelo Cuartas. Recorded April 2024 at UCLA Herb Alpert School of Music Studio, Los Angeles, California. Mixed and mastered by Jose Carrillo and Joel Eglash. Recordings sponsored by and coordinated with the Lowell Milken Center for Music of American Jewish Experience (UCLA) (Dr. Mark Kligman, Dr. David Brown, and Sharyl Holtzman). Instrumentalists performed in cooperation with UCLA Herb Alpert School of Music.

KOL HAN'SHAMAH כל הנשמה

BAND VOLUME II

Full Score

Adon Olam

אדון עולם

Text: **Liturgy**

Music: Traditional

Arranged by **Emily Tummons**
Corresponding choral arrangement by **Susan Lewis Friedman**
Piano arranged by **Susan Lewis Friedman** and **Gregory Shifrin**

Corresponding choral arrangement available in *Kol Han'shamah: Choir Volume II* (TMP 994068)

Mel.
1
2
Bass
Pno.
Last time to Coda
Last time to Coda
kol, a - zai Me - lech sh' - mo nik - ra, a - don o - lam. 1. V' - 2. V' - 3. V' -
VERSES
a - cha - rei kich - lot ha - kol, l' - va - do yim - loch no - ra, a - don o - lam. V'-
hu e - chad v' - ein shei - ni, l' - ham - shil lo l' - hach - bi - rah, a - don o - lam. B'-
hu Ei - li v' - chai go - a - li, v' - tzur chev - li b' - eit tza - rah, a - don o - lam. V'-
4. B' - ya - do af - kid ru - chi, b' - eit i - shan v' - a - i - rah, a - don o - lam. V'-
mf
mf

Fm Bb7 Fm Bb7 Bb Bb7/D Eb Bb7 Eb
1.-3. D.S.
4. D.S. al Coda
15
Mel.
hu ha - yah, v' - hu ho - veh, v' - hu yih'-yeh, b'-tif - a - rah, a - don o - lam. A - don o -
li rei - shit b' - li tach - lit, v' - lo ha - oz v' - ha - mis - rah, a - don o - lam. A - don o -
hu ni - si u - ma - nos li, m' - nat ko - si b'-yom ek - ra, a - don o - lam. A - don o -
im ru - chi g' - vi - ya - ti, A - do - nai li v' - lo i - ra, a - don o - lam. A - don o -
1
2
Bass
Pno.
1.-3. D.S.
4. D.S. al Coda

𝄌 CODA

Bb7 Eb Bb7 Eb
19
non-rit.
Mel.
zai Me - lech sh' - mo nik - ra, a - don o - lam.
1
2
Bass
Pno.
non-rit.

You are our Eternal God,
who reigned before any being had been created;
when all was done according to Your will,
then You were called Ruler.

And after all ceases to be,
You alone will rule in majesty.
You have been, are yet,
and will be in glory.

And You are One;
none other can compare to or consort with You.
You are without beginning, without end.
To You belong power and dominion.

And You are my God, my living Redeemer,
my Rock in times of trouble and distress.
You are my standard bearer and my refuge,
my benefactor when I call on You.

Into Your hands I entrust my spirit,
when I sleep and when I wake,
and with my spirit my body also;
Adonai is with me and I shall not fear.

אֲדוֹן עוֹלָם אֲשֶׁר מָלַךְ,
בְּטֶֽרֶם כָּל יְצִיר נִבְרָא.
לְעֵת נַעֲשָׂה בְחֶפְצוֹ כֹּל,
אֲזַי מֶֽלֶךְ שְׁמוֹ נִקְרָא.

וְאַחֲרֵי כִּכְלוֹת הַכֹּל,
לְבַדּוֹ יִמְלוֹךְ נוֹרָא.
וְהוּא הָיָה, וְהוּא הֹוֶה,
וְהוּא יִהְיֶה, בְּתִפְאָרָה.

וְהוּא אֶחָד וְאֵין שֵׁנִי,
לְהַמְשִׁיל לוֹ לְהַחְבִּֽירָה.
בְּלִי רֵאשִׁית בְּלִי תַכְלִית,
וְלוֹ הָעֹז וְהַמִּשְׂרָה.

וְהוּא אֵלִי וְחַי גֹּאֲלִי,
וְצוּר חֶבְלִי בְּעֵת צָרָה.
וְהוּא נִסִּי וּמָנוֹס לִי,
מְנָת כּוֹסִי בְּיוֹם אֶקְרָא.

בְּיָדוֹ אַפְקִיד רוּחִי,
בְּעֵת אִישַׁן וְאָעִֽירָה.
וְעִם רוּחִי גְּוִיָּתִי,
יְיָ לִי וְלֹא אִירָא.

Piano / Vocal

Adon Olam

אדון עולם

Text: **Liturgy**

Music: Traditional

Corresponding band arrangement by **Emily Tummons**
Corresponding choral arrangement by **Susan Lewis Friedman**
Piano arranged by **Susan Lewis Friedman** and **Gregory Shifrin**

Corresponding choral arrangement available in *Kol Han'shamah: Choir Volume II* (TMP 994068)

VERSES
E♭ B♭(omit3) E♭ B♭(omit3) E♭ Fm Fm7 B♭
a - cha - rei kich - lot ha - kol, l' - va - do yim - loch no - ra, a - don o - lam. V'
hu e - chad v' - ein shei - ni, l' - ham - shil lo l' - hach - bi - rah, a - don o - lam. B'-
hu Ei - li v' - chai go - a - li, v' - tzur chev - li b' - eit tza - rah, a - don o - lam. V'
4. B' - ya - do af - kid ru - chi, b' - eit i - shan v' - a - i - rah, a - don o - lam. V'
Fm B♭7 Fm B♭7 B♭ B♭7/D E♭ B♭7 E♭
1.-3. D.S.
4. D.S. al Coda
hu ha - yah, v' - hu ho - veh, v' - hu yih' - yeh, b' - tif - a - rah, a - don o - lam. A - don o -
li rei - shit b' - li tach - lit, v' - lo ha - oz v' - ha - mis - rah, a - don o - lam. A - don o -
hu ni - si u - ma - nos li, m' - nat ko - si b' - yom ek - ra, a - don o - lam. A - don o -
im ru - chi g' - vi - ya - ti, A - do - nai li v' - lo i - ra, a - don o - lam. A - don o -
CODA
B♭7 E♭ B♭7 E♭
non-rit.
zai Me - lech sh' - mo nik - ra, a - don o - lam.

Lead Sheet / Melody for C Instruments

Adon Olam

אדון עולם

Text: **Liturgy**

Music: Traditional

Arranged by **Emily Tummons**
Corresponding choral arrangement by **Susan Lewis Friedman**

Corresponding choral arrangement available in *Kol Han'shamah: Choir Volume II* (TMP 994068)

Melody for B♭ Instruments

Adon Olam

אדון עולם

Music: Traditional

Arranged by **Emily Tummons**

Corresponding choral arrangement available in *Kol Han'shamah: Choir Volume II* (TMP 994068)

Melody for E♭ Instruments

Adon Olam

אדון עולם

Music: Traditional

Arranged by **Emily Tummons**

Corresponding choral arrangement available in *Kol Han'shamah: Choir Volume II* (TMP 994068)

Melody for Bass Clef Instruments

Adon Olam

אדון עולם

Music: Traditional

Arranged by **Emily Tummons**

Corresponding choral arrangement available in *Kol Han'shamah: Choir Volume II* (TMP 994068)

Parts 1 and 2 for C Instruments

Adon Olam

אדון עולם

Music: Traditional

Arranged by **Emily Tummons**

Corresponding choral arrangement available in *Kol Han'shamah: Choir Volume II* (TMP 994068)

𝄌 *CODA*

Parts 1 and 2 for B♭ Instruments

Adon Olam

אדון עולם

Music: Traditional

Arranged by **Emily Tummons**

Corresponding choral arrangement available in *Kol Han'shamah: Choir Volume II* (TMP 994068)

𝄌 *CODA*

Parts 1 and 2 for E♭ Instruments

Adon Olam

אדון עולם

Music: Traditional

Arranged by **Emily Tummons**

Corresponding choral arrangement available in *Kol Han'shamah: Choir Volume II* (TMP 994068)

𝄌 *CODA*

Bass

Adon Olam

אדון עולם

Music: Traditional

Arranged by **Emily Tummons**

Corresponding choral arrangement available in *Kol Han'shamah: Choir Volume II* (TMP 994068)

Full Score

Ahavat Olam

אהבת עולם

Text: **Evening liturgy**

Music: **Eric Mandell**

Arranged by **Emily Tummons**
Piano arrangement and corresponding choral arrangement
by **Rachelle Nelson**

Lightly; with a lilt ♩. = 52
Small notes indicate optional solo treble instrument

Corresponding choral arrangement available in *Kol Han'shamah: Choir Volume II* (TMP 994068)

Em
B Em
E7
Am
D
D7
G
Mel.
ta. Al kein, A - do - nai E - lo - hei - nu, b'-shoch - bei - nu u - v - ku - mei - nu na -
1
mf
2
mf
Bass
Pno.

Cmaj7
D7
G
B7
Em
E7
Am
Mel.
si - ach, b'-chu - ke - cha, v'-nis - mach b'- div - rei To - ra - te - cha
1
2
Bass
Pno.

19
D D7 G Cmaj7 B7 Em
Mel.
u - v - mitz - vo - te - cha l' - o - lam va - ed. Ki
1
mp
2
mp
Bass
Pno.
C
23
Em A Am Em C D7 G B7
Mel.
heim cha - yei - nu v' - o - rech ya - mei - nu u - va -
1
2
Bass
Pno.

Everlasting love
You offered Your people Israel
by teaching us Torah and mitzvot,
laws and precepts.
Therefore, Adonai our God,
when we lie down and when we rise up,
we will meditate on Your laws
and Your commandments.
We will rejoice in Your Torah forever.
Day and night we will reflect on them
for they are our life and doing them lengths our days.

אַהֲבַת עוֹלָם
בֵּית יִשְׂרָאֵל עַמְּךָ אָהָבְתָּ,
תּוֹרָה וּמִצְוֹת,
חֻקִּים וּמִשְׁפָּטִים, אוֹתָנוּ לִמַּדְתָּ.
עַל כֵּן, יְיָ אֱלֹהֵינוּ,
בְּשָׁכְבֵּנוּ וּבְקוּמֵנוּ
נָשִׂיחַ בְּחֻקֶּיךָ,
וְנִשְׂמַח בְּדִבְרֵי תוֹרָתֶךָ
וּבְמִצְוֹתֶיךָ לְעוֹלָם וָעֶד.
כִּי הֵם חַיֵּינוּ וְאֹרֶךְ יָמֵינוּ,
וּבָהֶם נֶהְגֶּה יוֹמָם וָלָיְלָה.

Piano / Vocal

Ahavat Olam

אהבת עולם

Text: **Evening liturgy**

Music: **Eric Mandell**

Corresponding band arrangement by **Emily Tummons**
Piano arrangement and corresponding choral arrangement
by **Rachelle Nelson**

Corresponding choral arrangement available in *Kol Han'shamah: Choir Volume II* (TMP 994068)

15
Cmaj7 D7 G B7 Em E7 Am
si - ach, b'-chu-ke - cha, v'-nis-mach b'-div-rei To-ra-te - cha
19
D D7 G Cmaj7 B7 Em
u - v - mitz - vo - te - cha l'-o - lam va - ed. Ki
C
23
Em A Am Em C D7 G B7
heim cha - yei - nu v'-o-rech ya-mei - nu u-va-
27
Em A Am Em C B7 Em
rit.
hem neh - geh yo-mam va-lai - lah.
rit.

Lead Sheet / Melody for C Instruments

Ahavat Olam

אהבת עולם

Text: **Evening liturgy**

Music: **Eric Mandell**

Arranged by **Emily Tummons**
Corresponding choral arrangement by **Rachelle Nelson**

Corresponding choral arrangement available in *Kol Han'shamah: Choir Volume II* (TMP 994068)

Melody for B♭ Instruments

Ahavat Olam

אהבת עולם

Music: **Eric Mandell**

Arranged by **Emily Tummons**

Corresponding choral arrangement available in *Kol Han'shamah: Choir Volume II* (TMP 994068)

Melody for E♭ Instruments

Ahavat Olam

אהבת עולם

Music: **Eric Mandell**

Arranged by **Emily Tummons**

Corresponding choral arrangement available in *Kol Han'shamah: Choir Volume II* (TMP 994068)

Melody for Bass Clef Instruments

Ahavat Olam

אהבת עולם

Music: **Eric Mandell**

Arranged by **Emily Tummons**

Corresponding choral arrangement available in *Kol Han'shamah: Choir Volume II* (TMP 994068)

Parts 1 and 2 for C Instruments

Ahavat Olam

אהבת עולם

Music: **Eric Mandell**

Arranged by **Emily Tummons**

Corresponding choral arrangement available in *Kol Han'shamah: Choir Volume II* (TMP 994068)

Ki heim...
C
rit.
rit.

Parts 1 and 2 for B♭ Instruments

Ahavat Olam

אהבת עולם

Music: **Eric Mandell**

Arranged by **Emily Tummons**

Corresponding choral arrangement available in *Kol Han'shamah: Choir Volume II* (TMP 994068)

19
1.
2
Ki heim...
mp
mp
C
23
1.
2
27
p
rit.
rit.
1.
2
p
p

Parts 1 and 2 for E♭ Instruments

Ahavat Olam

אהבת עולם

Music: **Eric Mandell**

Arranged by **Emily Tummons**

Lightly; with a lilt ♩. = 52

Small notes indicate optional solo treble instrument

Corresponding choral arrangement available in *Kol Han'shamah: Choir Volume II* (TMP 994068)

19
1
2
Ki heim...
mp
mp
C
23
27
p
rit.
rit.
p
p

Bass

Ahavat Olam

אהבת עולם

Music: **Eric Mandell**

Arranged by **Emily Tummons**

Corresponding choral arrangement available in *Kol Han'shamah: Choir Volume II* (TMP 994068)

Full Score

Bar'chu

ברכו

Text: **Liturgy**

Music: **Rachelle Nelson**

Arranged by **Emily Tummons**
Corresponding choral arrangement by **Rachelle Nelson**
Piano arranged by **Rachelle Nelson** and **Gregory Shifrin**

In moderate three ♩ = 116
Small notes indicate optional solo treble instrument

Corresponding choral arrangement available in *Kol Han'shamah: Choir Volume II* (TMP 994068)

Dm G G/B B♭(add9) C
Mel.
Yai lai lai lai lai lai lai, lai lai lai lai lai lai
1
2
Bass
Pno.
Dm C/D Dm C7 B F C A A7
lai. Lai lai lai lai lai lai lai lai lai lai lai lai lai
mf
mf

25
B♭ C F C7 F
Mel.
lai lai lai lai lai lai. Lai lai lai lai lai lai lai
1
2
Bass
Pno.
31
C A A7 B♭ C Am7 Dm C/D Dm C/D
Mel.
lai lai lai lai lai lai lai lai lai.
1
2
Bass
Pno.

C
Dm G G/B B♭(add9) C
Mel.
Ba - r' - chu et A - do - nai ha - m - vo -
1
2
Bass
Pno.
Dm C/D Dm C7 F C A A7
rach! Ba - ruch A - do - nai ha - m - vo - rach
mf
mf

49
Mel.
1
2
Bass
Pno.
B♭ C F C7 F
l' - o - lam va - ed. Ba - ruch A - do - nai
55
C A A7 B♭ C Am7 Dm C/D Dm C/D
ha - m - vo - rach l' - o - lam va - ed!

D
Dm
G
G/B
B♭(add9)
61
Mel.
Lai lai lai lai lai lai lai, lai lai lai
1
mp
2
mp
Bass
Pno.

C
Dm
C/D
Dm
C/D
Dm
66
Mel.
lai lai lai lai. Yai lai lai
1
p
2
p
Bass
Pno.

Praise Adonai to whom praise is due forever!
Praised be Adonai to whom praise is due, now and forever!

בָּרְכוּ אֶת יְיָ הַמְבֹרָךְ!
בָּרוּךְ יְיָ הַמְבֹרָךְ לְעוֹלָם וָעֶד!

Piano / Vocal

Bar'chu

ברכו

Text: **Liturgy**

Music: **Rachelle Nelson**

Corresponding band arrangement by **Emily Tummons**
Corresponding choral arrangement by **Rachelle Nelson**
Piano arranged by **Rachelle Nelson** and **Gregory Shifrin**

In moderate three ♩ = 116

Corresponding choral arrangement available in *Kol Han'shamah: Choir Volume II* (TMP 994068)

19
Dm C/D Dm C7 B F C A A7
lai. Lai lai lai lai lai lai lai lai lai lai lai lai lai
25
B♭ C F C7 F
lai lai lai lai lai lai. Lai lai lai lai lai lai lai
31
C A A7 B♭ C Am7 Dm C/D Dm C/D
lai lai lai lai lai lai lai lai lai.

C
Dm G G/B B♭(add9) C
Ba - r' - chu et A - do - nai ha - m - vo -
Dm C/D Dm C7 F C A A7
rach! Ba - ruch A - do - nai ha - m - vo - rach
B♭ C F C7 F
l' - o - lam va - ed. Ba - ruch A - do - nai

55
C A A7 B♭ C Am7 Dm C/D Dm C/D
ha - m - vo - rach l' - o - lam va - ed!
D
61
Dm G G/B B♭(add9)
Lai lai lai lai lai lai lai, lai lai lai
66
C Dm C/D Dm C/D Dm
lai lai lai lai. Yai lai lai
71
G G/B B♭(add9) C Am7 Dm C/D Dm(add9)
rit.
lai lai lai lai, lai lai lai lai lai lai lai.
rit.

Lead Sheet / Melody for C Instruments

Bar'chu

ברכו

Text: **Liturgy**

Music: **Rachelle Nelson**
Arranged by **Emily Tummons**
Corresponding choral arrangement by **Rachelle Nelson**

Corresponding choral arrangement available in *Kol Han'shamah: Choir Volume II* (TMP 994068)

C
Ba - r' - chu et A - do - nai ha - m' - vo - rach!
Ba - ruch A - do - nai ha - m - vo - rach l' - o - lam va - ed.
Ba - ruch A - do - nai ha - m - vo - rach l' - o - lam va - ed!
D
Lai lai lai lai lai lai lai, lai lai lai
lai lai lai lai.
Yai lai lai
lai lai lai lai, lai lai lai lai lai lai lai.
rit.

Melody for B♭ Instruments

Bar'chu

ברכו

Music: **Rachelle Nelson**
Arranged by **Emily Tummons**

Corresponding choral arrangement available in *Kol Han'shamah: Choir Volume II* (TMP 994068)

55
D
Lai lai lai...
63
71
rit.

Melody for E♭ Instruments

Bar'chu

ברכו

Music: **Rachelle Nelson**
Arranged by **Emily Tummons**

In moderate three ♩ **= 116**

Corresponding choral arrangement available in *Kol Han'shamah: Choir Volume II* (TMP 994068)

55
D
Lai lai lai...
63
71
rit.

Melody for Bass Clef Instruments

Bar'chu

ברכו

Music: **Rachelle Nelson**
Arranged by **Emily Tummons**

Corresponding choral arrangement available in *Kol Han'shamah: Choir Volume II* (TMP 994068)

55
D
Lai lai lai...
63
71
rit.

Parts 1 and 2 for C Instruments

Bar'chu

ברכו

Music: **Rachelle Nelson**

Arranged by **Emily Tummons**

In moderate three ♩ = 116

Small notes indicate optional solo treble instrument

Corresponding choral arrangement available in *Kol Han'shamah: Choir Volume II* (TMP 994068)

23
1
2
28
1
2
C
33
Bar'chu...
1
2
38
1
2
45
1
mf
2
mf

50
56
60
D
Lai lai lai...
65
71
rit.
rit.

Parts 1 and 2 for B♭ Instruments

Bar'chu

ברכו

Music: **Rachelle Nelson**

Arranged by **Emily Tummons**

Corresponding choral arrangement available in *Kol Han'shamah: Choir Volume II* (TMP 994068)

23
28
33
C
Bar'chu...
38
45
mf
mf

D
Lai lai lai...
rit.
rit.

Parts 1 and 2 for E♭ Instruments

Bar'chu

ברכו

Music: **Rachelle Nelson**

Arranged by **Emily Tummons**

Corresponding choral arrangement available in *Kol Han'shamah: Choir Volume II* (TMP 994068)

28
1
2
33
C
Bar'chu...
38
45
mf
50
f

D
Lai lai lai...
rit.
rit.

Bass

Bar'chu

ברכו

Music: **Rachelle Nelson**

Arranged by **Emily Tummons**

Corresponding choral arrangement available in *Kol Han'shamah: Choir Volume II* (TMP 994068)

45
F C A A7 B♭ C
51
F C7 F C A A7
57
B♭ C Am7 Dm C/D Dm C/D
D
Dm
Lai lai lai...
63
G G/B B♭(add9) C Dm C/D Dm C/D Dm
70
G G/B B♭(add9) C Am7 Dm C/D Dm(add9)
rit.

Full Score

L'chah Dodi

לכה דודי

Text: **Shlomo Alkabetz ben HaLevi (16th C.)**

Music: **Aaron Bensoussan**

Arranged by **Emily Tummons**
Piano arrangement and corresponding choral arrangement
by **Robbie Solomon**

Corresponding choral arrangement available in *Kol Han'shamah: Choir Volume II* (TMP 994068)

Em D C B7 Em B7
Mel.
lai. Yal la lai lai ya la lai lai ya la lai lai la la la la lai. L'-
1
2
Bass
Pno.
B Em Am7 B7 F♯m7(♭5) B7 Em B7
chah do-di li-k-rat ka-lah, p'-nei Shab-bat n'-ka-b'-lah. L'-

Em Am7 B F#m7(b5) B F#m7(b5) B7 Em D
Mel.
chah do - di li - k-rat ka - lah, p' - nei Shab-bat n' - ka - b' - lah. 1. Sha - 2. Lik - 5. Hit -
1
2
Bass
Pno.
C
G Am D Am B7
mor v' - za - chor b' - di - bur e - chad, hish - mi - a - nu Eil
rat Shab - bat l' - chu v' - neil' - chah, ki hi m' - kor ha -
o - r' - ri, hit - o - r' - ri, ki va o - reich,
Parts I & II optional tacet on Verses 1 and 2
mp

Em D G Am D
19
Mel.
ham' - yu - chad, A - do - nai e - chad u - sh - mo e - chad,
b'ra - chah, mei - rosh mi - ke - dem n' - su - chah,
ku - mi o - ri, u - ri u - ri shir da - bei - ri,
1
2
Bass
Pno.
1. 2. Am F♯m7(♭5) B B7 Em 3. Am F♯m7(♭5) B
22
Mel.
l'-sheim ul - tif - e - ret v' - li - t - hi - lah. L' - k'vod A - do - nai a -
sof ma - a - seh b' - macha - sha - vah t'chi - lah. L' -
1
2
Bass
Pno.

25
B7 Em D Em Am7 B F#m7(b5) B7
Mel.
la - yich nig - lah. L' - chah do - di li - k-rat ka - lah, p' - nei Shab - bat
1
mf
2
mf
Bass
Pno.
29
Em Am7 B F#m7(b5) B7 F#m7(b5) B7 Em
Mel.
n'-ka - b'-lah. L'-chah do-di li - k-rat ka - lah, p' nei Shab-bat n' - ka - b'-lah.
1
2
Bass
Pno.

E
Em
D
Cmaj7
B7
Mel.
Ya la lai lai, ya la lai lai, ya la lai lai, la la lai lai
small note may be played an octave lower
1
2
Bass
Pno.
Em
D
C
B
Em
D7
poco rit.
Piu lento
lai, ya la lai lai, ya la lai lai, ya la lai lai, la la lai lai lai. 9. Bo -
poco rit.
Piu lento

F
G Am D7 Am B7 Em D G
Mel.
i v'-sha-lom a-te-ret ba-lah, gam b'-sim-chah uv-tzo-ho-lah,
1
mp
2
Bass
Pno.
Am D7 Am7 B7 Tempo I Em
Mel.
toch e-mu-nei am s'-gu-lah, bo-i cha-lah, bo-i cha-lah. L'-
1
tutti
f
2
f
Bass
Tempo I
Pno.

G
Em Am7 B F#m7(b5) B7 Em
Mel.
chah do-di li - k-rat ka-lah, p'-nei Shab-bat n'-ka-b'-lah. L' -
small note ad lib
1
2
Bass
Pno.
Am7 B F#m7(b5) B7 F#m7(b5) B7 Em
chah do-di li - k-rat ka-lah, p'-nei Shab-bat n' - ka - b'-lah.

Beloved, come to meet the bride;
beloved, come to greet Shabbat.

לְכָה דוֹדִי לִקְרַאת כַּלָּה,
פְּנֵי שַׁבָּת נְקַבְּלָה.

1. "Keep" and "remember": a single command
the Only God caused us to hear;
the Eternal is One, God's name is One;
glory and praise are God's.

1. שָׁמוֹר וְזָכוֹר בְּדִבּוּר אֶחָד,
הִשְׁמִיעָנוּ אֵל הַמְיֻחָד,
יְיָ אֶחָד וּשְׁמוֹ אֶחָד,
לְשֵׁם וּלְתִפְאֶרֶת וְלִתְהִלָּה.

2. Come with me to meet Shabbat,
forever a fountain of blessing.
Still it flows, as from the start:
the last of days, for which the first was made.

2. לִקְרַאת שַׁבָּת לְכוּ וְנֵלְכָה,
כִּי הִיא מְקוֹר הַבְּרָכָה,
מֵרֹאשׁ מִקֶּדֶם נְסוּכָה,
סוֹף מַעֲשֶׂה בְּמַחֲשָׁבָה תְּחִלָּה.

5. Awake, awake,
your light has come!
Arise, shine, awake, and sing:
the Eternal's glory dawns upon you.

5. הִתְעוֹרְרִי, הִתְעוֹרְרִי,
כִּי בָא אוֹרֵךְ, קוּמִי אוֹרִי,
עוּרִי עוּרִי, שִׁיר דַּבֵּרִי,
כְּבוֹד יְיָ עָלַיִךְ נִגְלָה.

9. Enter in peace, O crown of your husband;
enter in gladness, enter in joy.
Come to the people that keeps its faith.
Enter, O bride! Enter, O bride!

9. בּוֹאִי בְשָׁלוֹם עֲטֶרֶת בַּעְלָהּ,
גַּם בְּשִׂמְחָה וּבְצָהֳלָה,
תּוֹךְ אֱמוּנֵי עַם סְגֻלָּה,
בּוֹאִי כַלָּה, בּוֹאִי כַלָּה.

Piano / Vocal

L'chah Dodi

לכה דודי

Text: **Shlomo Alkabetz ben HaLevi (16th C.)**

Music: **Aaron Bensoussan**

Corresponding band arrangement by **Emily Tummons**
Piano arrangement and corresponding choral arrangement
by **Robbie Solomon**

Corresponding choral arrangement available in *Kol Han'shamah: Choir Volume II* (TMP 994068)

Am7 B7 F#m7(b5) B7 Em B7 Em
li - k-rat ka-lah, p'-nei Shab-bat n'-ka-b'-lah. L'-chah do-di
Am7 B F#m7(b5) B F#m7(b5) B7 Em D
li - k-rat ka-lah, p'-nei Shab-bat n' - ka - b'-lah.
1. Sha-
2. Lik -
5. Hit -
C
G Am D Am B7
mor v'-za-chor b'-di-bur e-chad, hish-mi-a - nu Eil
rat Shab-bat l'-chu v'-neil'-chah, ki hi m'-kor ha-
o - r'-ri, hit - o - r'-ri, ki va o-reich,

19
Em D G Am D
ham' - yu-chad, A-do-nai e-chad u-sh-mo e-chad,
b'ra - chah, mei - rosh mi-ke - dem n'-su - chah,
ku-mi o - ri, u - ri u - ri shir da-bei - ri,
22
1. 2. Am F#m7(b5) B B7 Em
l'-sheim ul-tif-e - ret v'-li-t-hi - lah. L'-
sof ma-a-seh b'-macha-sha-vah t'chi-lah. L'-
3. Am F#m7(b5) B
k'vod A-do-nai a-
25
B7 Em
la-yich nig - lah.
D
Em Am7 B F#m7(b5) B7
L'-chah do-di li-k-rat ka-lah, p'-nei Shab-bat

29
Em Am7 B F#m7(b5) B7
n'-ka-b'-lah. L'-chah do-di li-k-rat ka-lah, p'-nei Shab-bat n'-
33
F#m7(b5) B7 Em
E
Em D Cmaj7 B7
ka-b' lah. Ya la lai lai, ya la lai lai, ya la lai lai, la la lai lai
36
Em D C B Em D7
poco rit.
Piu lento
lai, ya la lai lai, ya la lai lai, ya la lai lai, la la lai lai lai. 9. Bo-
poco rit.
Piu lento

F
39
G Am D7 Am B7 Em D G
i v'-sha-lom a - te - ret ba - lah, gam b'-sim-chah uv - tzo - ho-lah,
43
Am D7 Am7 B7 Tempo I Em
toch e-mu-nei am s'-gu - lah, bo - i cha-lah, bo - i cha-lah. L'-
Tempo I
G
47
Em Am7 B F#m7(b5) B7 Em
chah do-di li - k-rat ka-lah, p'-nei Shab-bat n'-ka - b'-lah. L'-
51
Am7 B F#m7(b5) B7 F#m7(b5) B7 Em
chah do-di li - k-rat ka-lah, p'-nei Shab-bat n' - ka - b'-lah.

Lead Sheet / Melody for C Instruments

L'chah Dodi

לכה דודי

Text: **Shlomo Alkabetz ben HaLevi (16th C.)**

Music: **Aaron Bensoussan**

Arranged by **Emily Tummons**
Corresponding choral arrangement by **Robbie Solomon**

Corresponding choral arrangement available in *Kol Han'shamah: Choir Volume II* (TMP 994068)

1. 2. Am F#m7(b5) B B7 Em
3. Am F#m7(b5) B B7 Em
l'-sheim ul-tif-e-ret v'-li-t-hi-lah. L'-
sof ma-a-seh b'-macha-sha-vah t'chi-lah. L'-
k'vod A-do-nai a-la-yich nig-lah. L'-
D Em Am7 B F#m7(b5) B7 Em
chah do-di li-k-rat ka-lah, p'-nei Shab-bat n'-ka-b'-lah. L'-chah do-di
Am7 B F#m7(b5) B7 F#m7(b5) B7 Em E Em D
li-k-rat ka-lah, p' nei Shab-bat n'-ka-b'-lah. Ya la lai lai, ya la lai
Cmaj7 B7 Em D
lai, ya la lai lai, la la lai lai lai, ya la lai lai, ya la lai
C B Em D7 F G Am D7
poco rit.
Piu lento
lai, ya la lai lai, la la lai lai lai. 9. Bo-i v'-sha-lom a-te-ret ba-lah,
Am B7 Em D G Am D7 Am7 B7
gam b'-sim-chah uv-tzo-ho-lah, toch e-mu-nei am s'-gu-lah, bo-i cha-lah,
Tempo I Em G Em Am7 B F#m7(b5) B7 Em
bo-i cha-lah. L'-chah do-di li-k-rat ka-lah, p'-nei Shab-bat n'-ka-b'-lah. L'-
Am7 B F#m7(b5) B7 F#m7(b5) B7 Em
chah do-di li-k-rat ka-lah, p'-nei Shab-bat n'-ka-b'-lah.

Melody for B♭ Instruments

L'chah Dodi

לכה דודי

Music: **Aaron Bensoussan**

Arranged by **Emily Tummons**

Corresponding choral arrangement available in *Kol Han'shamah: Choir Volume II* (TMP 994068)

D
E
Ya la lai...
poco rit.
Piu lento
Boi v'shalom...
F
Tempo I
L'chah...
G

Melody for E♭ Instruments

L'chah Dodi

לכה דודי

Music: **Aaron Bensoussan**

Arranged by **Emily Tummons**

Corresponding choral arrangement available in *Kol Han'shamah: Choir Volume II* (TMP 994068)

D
E
Ya la lai...
poco rit.
Piu lento
Boi v'shalom...
F
Tempo I
L'chah...
G

Melody for Bass Clef Instruments

L'chah Dodi

לכה דודי

Music: **Aaron Bensoussan**

Arranged by **Emily Tummons**

Corresponding choral arrangement available in *Kol Han'shamah: Choir Volume II* (TMP 994068)

D
26
30
E
34
Ya la lai...
36
poco rit.
Piu lento
Boi v'shalom...
F
39
43
Tempo I
L'chah...
G
47
51

Parts 1 and 2 for C Instruments

L'chah Dodi

לכה דודי

Music: **Aaron Bensoussan**

Arranged by **Emily Tummons**

Corresponding choral arrangement available in *Kol Han'shamah: Choir Volume II* (TMP 994068)

C
1. Shamor v'zachor... 2. Likrat Shabbat... 5. Hitor'ri...
Parts I & II optional tacet on Verses 1 and 2
Parts I & II optional tacet on Verses 1 and 2
1. 2.
3.
D
L'chah...
E
small note may be played an octave lower
Ya la lai...

poco rit.
F
Piu lento
Boi v'shalom...
poco rit.
mp
Tempo I
L'chah...
tutti
f
f
G
small note ad lib

Parts 1 and 2 for B♭ Instruments

L'chah Dodi

לכה דודי

Music: **Aaron Bensoussan**

Arranged by **Emily Tummons**

Corresponding choral arrangement available in *Kol Han'shamah: Choir Volume II* (TMP 994068)

C
1. Shamor v'zachor... 2. Likrat Shabbat... 5. Hitor'ri...
Parts I & II optional tacet on Verses 1 and 2
16
1
mp
Parts I & II optional tacet on Verses 1 and 2
2
mp
20
1. 2.
3.
24
L'chah...
D
mf
mf
28
32
Ya la lai...
E
small note may be played an octave lower

36
poco rit.
F
Piu lento
Boi v'shalom...
poco rit.
42
Tempo I
L'chah...
mp
tutti
f
f
G
small note ad lib
47
50
53

Parts 1 and 2 for B♭ Instruments

L'chah Dodi

לכה דודי

Music: **Aaron Bensoussan**

Arranged by **Emily Tummons**

Corresponding choral arrangement available in *Kol Han'shamah: Choir Volume II* (TMP 994068)

C
1. Shamor v'zachor... 2. Likrat Shabbat... 5. Hitor'ri...
Parts I & II optional tacet on Verses 1 and 2
Parts I & II optional tacet on Verses 1 and 2
1. 2.
3.
D
L'chah...
E
small note may be played an octave lower
Ya la lai...

poco rit.
F
Piu lento
Boi v'shalom...
mp
Tempo I
L'chah...
tutti
f
G
small note ad lib

Bass

L'chah Dodi

לכה דודי

Music: **Aaron Bensoussan**

Arranged by **Emily Tummons**

Corresponding choral arrangement available in *Kol Han'shamah: Choir Volume II* (TMP 994068)

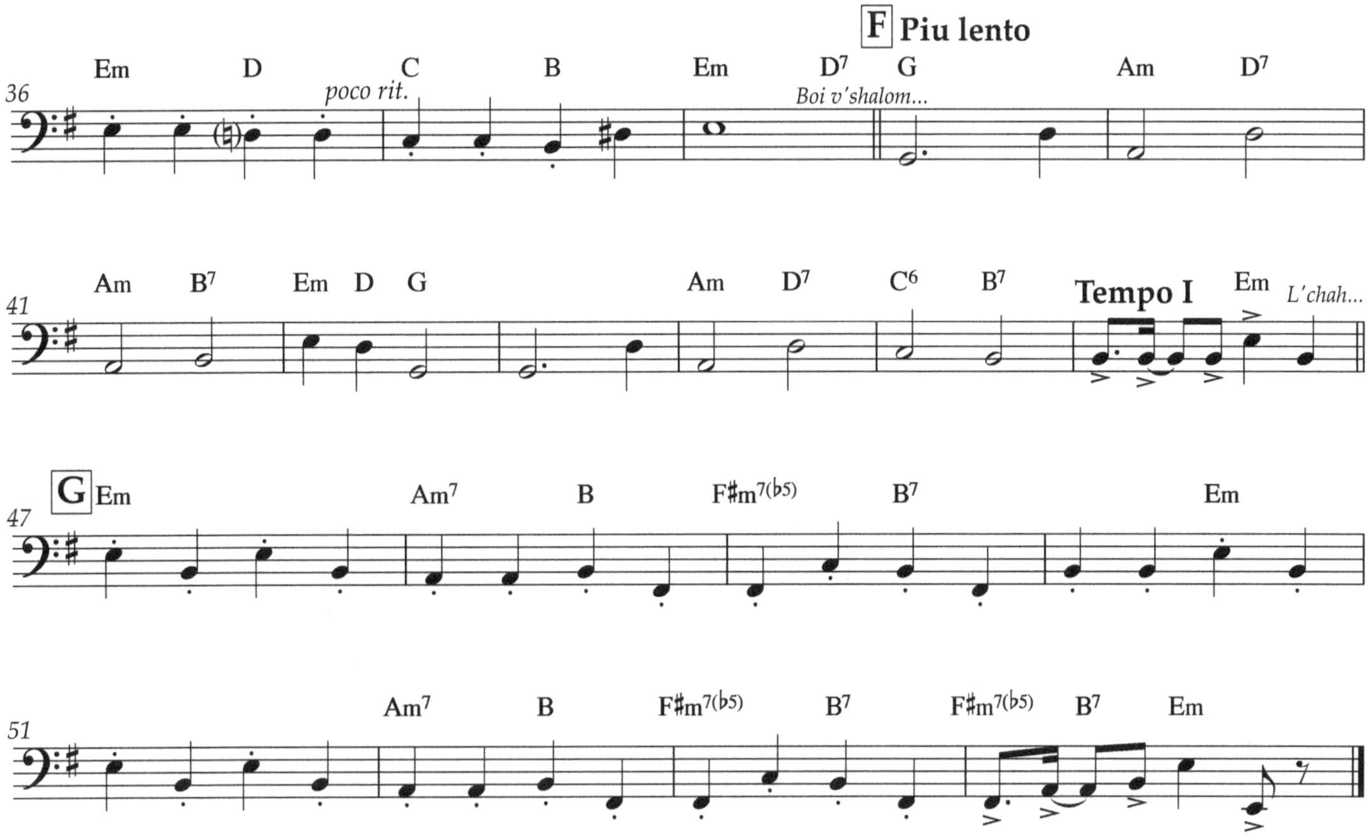
F Piu lento
Em D C B Em D7 G Am D7
36
poco rit.
Boi v'shalom...
Am B7 Em D G Am D7 C6 B7 Em
41
Tempo I
L'chah...
G Em Am7 B F#m7(b5) B7 Em
47
Am7 B F#m7(b5) B7 F#m7(b5) B7 Em
51

Full Score

Light One Candle

Music and text: **Peter Yarrow**

Arranged by **Emily Tummons**
Corresponding choral arrangement by **Susan Lewis Friedman** and **David Berger**
Piano arranged by **Susan Lewis Friedman** and **Gregory Shifrin**

Upbeat folk style ♩ = 120
Small notes indicate optional solo treble instrument

9
Ab/G Fm Fm/Eb Db
Mel.
thanks that their light did - n't die. Light one can-dle for the pain they en-dured_ when their
1
mp
2
mp
Bass
Pno.

13
C7 Fm Fm/Eb
Mel.
mf
right to ex - ist was de - nied. Light one can-dle for the ter - ri - ble sac - ri - fice
1
mf
2
mf
Bass
Pno.

17
D♭ D♭/C B♭ A♭ Fm A♭ Fm
Mel.
jus-tice and free-dom de-mand. Light one can-dle for the wis-dom to know_ when the
1
2
Bass
Pno.
21
D♭ E♭7 A♭ C7
CHORUS
F7 B♭m
peace-mak-er's time is at hand._____ Don't let the light go out,__ it's
f

Mel.
1
2
Bass
Pno.
E♭7 A♭ C7 F7 B♭m
last-ed for so ma-ny years. Don't let the light go out, let it
E♭7 A♭ C7 Fm
shine through our love and our tears.

VERSE 2
Mel.
1
2
Bass
Pno.
Light one can - dle for the strength that we need to
nev - er be-come our own foe.
Light one can-dle for those who are suff' - ring the
A♭
A♭/G
Fm
Fm/E♭
D♭

Mel.
1
2
Bass
Pno.
C7 Fm Fm/E♭
pain we learned so long a - go. Light one can-dle for all we be-lieve_ in, that
mf
D♭ A♭/C B♭ A♭ Fm A♭ Fm
an - ger not tear us a - part. Light one can-dle to bind us to - geth - er, with

47
Db Eb7 Ab C7 CHORUS F7 Bbm
Mel.
peace as the song in our hearts. Don't let the light go out, it's
1
2
Bass
Pno.
51
Eb7 Ab C7 F7 Bbm
last-ed for so ma-ny years. Don't let the light go out, let it

55
Eb7
Ab
C
Fm
Mel.
shine through our love and our tears.
1
2
Bass
Pno.
VERSE 3
59
Ab
Ab/G
Fm
Fm/Eb
What is the mem - 'ry that's val-ued so high - ly that we keep a - live in that flame?
mp
mp

Mel.
1
2
Bass
Pno.
Db
C7
What's the com-mit - ment to those who have died_ that we cry out,"They've not died in vain"?
Fm
Fm/Eb
Db
Ab/C
Bb
We have come this_ far al-ways be-liev - ing that jus-tice would some-how pre - vail?
mf

71
Mel.
A♭ Fm A♭ Fm D♭ E♭7 A♭ C
This is the bur - den and this is the pro - mise and this is why we will not fail!
1
2
Bass
Pno.
CHORUS
75
F7 B♭m E♭7 A♭ C7
Don't let the light go out, it's last-ed for so ma-ny years.

79
F7
B♭m
E♭7
A♭
C7
Mel.
Don't let the light go out,___ let it shine through our love and our tears.___
1
2
Bass
Pno.
83
F7
B♭m
F7
B♭m
F7
B♭m
Mel.
Don't let the light go out.___ Don't let the light go out.___ Don't let the light go out!
1
2
Bass
Pno.

Piano / Vocal

Light One Candle

Music and text: **Peter Yarrow**

Corresponding band arrangement by **Emily Tummons**
Corresponding choral arrangement by **Susan Lewis Friedman** and **David Berger**
Piano arranged by **Susan Lewis Friedman** and **Gregory Shifrin**

Corresponding choral arrangement available in *Kol Han'shamah: Choir Volume II* (TMP 994068)

D♭
Light one can-dle for the pain they en-dured when their right to ex-ist was de-
C7 Fm mf Fm/E♭
nied. Light one can-dle for the ter-ri-ble sac-ri-fice
D♭ D♭/C B♭ A♭ Fm
jus-tice and free-dom de-mand. Light one can-dle for the

20
Ab Fm Db Eb7 Ab C7
wis-dom to know___ when the peace-mak-er's time is at hand.___
CHORUS
23
F7 Bbm Eb7
Don't let the light go out,___ it's last-ed for so___ ma-ny
26
Ab C7 F7 Bbm
years. Don't let the light go out,___ let it

Eb7 Ab C7 Fm
29
shine through our love and our tears.
VERSE 2 Ab Ab/G
f
33
Light one can-dle for the strength that we need to nev - er be-come our own
Fm Fm/Eb Db
36
foe. Light one can-dle for those who are suff' - ring the

39
C7
Fm
pain we learned so long a - go. Light one can-dle for
42
Fm/E♭
D♭
A♭/C
B♭
all we be - lieve in, that an - ger not tear us a - part.
45
A♭
Fm
A♭
Fm
D♭
E♭7
Light one can-dle to bind us to - geth - er, with peace as the song in our

48
A♭ C⁷ F⁷ CHORUS B♭m
hearts. Don't let the light go out, it's
51
E♭⁷ A♭ C⁷ F⁷
last - ed for so ma - ny years. Don't let the
54
B♭m E♭⁷ A♭ C
3 3
light go out, let it shine through our love and our tears.

Fm
VERSE 3
A♭
What is the mem - 'ry that's
A♭/G
Fm
Fm/E♭
val-ued so high - ly that we keep a - live in that flame?
D♭
What's the com-mit - ment to those who have died__ that we cry out,"They've not died in

66
C7
Fm
Fm/E♭
vain"? We have come this far al-ways be-liev-ing that
69
D♭
A♭/C
B♭
A♭
Fm
jus-tice would some-how pre-vail? This is the bur-den and
72
A♭
Fm
D♭
E♭7
A♭
C
this is the pro-mise and this is why we will not fail!

CHORUS
F7
Bbm
Eb7
Don't let the light go out, it's last-ed for so many
Ab
C7
years.
Don't let the light go out, let it
shine through our love and our tears.
Don't let the

84
B♭m
light go out.
F7
Don't let the light go out.
B♭m
87
F7
Don't let the light go out!
B♭m

Lead Sheet / Melody for C Instruments

Light One Candle

Music and text: **Peter Yarrow**

Arranged by **Emily Tummons**
Corresponding choral arrangement by **Susan Lewis Friedman** and **David Berger**

Corresponding choral arrangement available in *Kol Han'shamah: Choir Volume II* (TMP 994068)

D7 Eb7 G Ab B7 C7 Em Fm
shine through our love and our tears.
VERSE 2
G Ab G/F# Ab/G
Light one can - dle for the strength that we need to nev - er be - come our own
Em Fm Em/D Fm/Eb C Db
foe. Light one can-dle for those who are suff' - ring the pain we learned so long a -
B7 C7 Em Fm Em/D Fm/Eb C Db G/B Ab/C
go. Light one can-dle for all we be-lieve in, that an - ger not tear us a -
A Bb G Ab Em Fm G Ab Em Fm C Db D7 Eb7
part. Light one can-dle to bind us to - geth - er, with peace as the song in our
G Ab B7 C7 E7 F7 CHORUS Am Bbm D7 Eb7 G Ab B7 C7
hearts. Don't let the light go out, it's last-ed for so ma-ny years.
E7 F7 Am Bbm D7 Eb7 G Ab B C
Don't let the light go out, let it shine through our love and our tears.
Em Fm VERSE 3 G Ab
What is the mem - 'ry that's val-ued so high - ly that

G/F# Em Em/D C
Ab/G Fm Fm/Eb Db
we keep a - live in that flame? What's the com-mit - ment to those who have died that we
B7 Em Em/D
C7 Fm Fm/Eb
cry out,"They've not died in vain"? We have come this far al-ways be-liev - ing that
C G/B A G Em G Em
Db Ab/C Bb Ab Fm Ab Fm
jus - tice would some-how pre - vail? This is the bur - den and this is the pro - mise and
C D7 G B E7 Am
Db Eb7 Ab C F7 CHORUS Bbm
this is why we will not fail! Don't let the light go out, it's
D7 G B7 E7 Am
Eb7 Ab C7 F7 Bbm
last - ed for so ma - ny years. Don't let the light go out, let it
D7 G B7 E7 Am
Eb7 Ab C7 F7 Bbm
shine through our love and our tears. Don't let the light go out.
E7 Am E7 Am
F7 Bbm F7 Bbm
Don't let the light go out. Don't let the light go out!

Melody for B♭ Instruments

Light One Candle

Music: **Peter Yarrow**

Arranged by **Emily Tummons**

Corresponding choral arrangement available in *Kol Han'shamah: Choir Volume II* (TMP 994068)

Don't let the light go out...
CHORUS
What is the mem'ry...
VERSE 3
Don't let the light go out...
CHORUS

Melody for E♭ Instruments

Light One Candle

Music: **Peter Yarrow**

Arranged by **Emily Tummons**

Corresponding choral arrangement available in *Kol Han'shamah: Choir Volume II* (TMP 994068)

45
Don't let the light go out...
CHORUS
49
54
What is the mem'ry...
VERSE 3
59
63
67
71
Don't let the light go out...
CHORUS
75
79
83

Melody for Bass Clef Instruments

Light One Candle

Music: **Peter Yarrow**

Arranged by **Emily Tummons**

Corresponding choral arrangement available in *Kol Han'shamah: Choir Volume II* (TMP 994068)

45
Don't let the light go out...
CHORUS
49
54
What is the mem'ry...
VERSE 3
59
63
67
71
Don't let the light go out...
CHORUS
75
79
83

Parts 1 and 2 for C Instruments

Light One Candle

Music: **Peter Yarrow**

Arranged by **Emily Tummons**

Upbeat folk style ♩ = 120
Small notes indicate optional solo treble instrument

Corresponding choral arrangement available in *Kol Han'shamah: Choir Volume II* (TMP 994068)

25
1
2
3
30
mp
Light one candle...
VERSE 2
36
mf
42
48
Don't let the light go out...
CHORUS
f

What is the mem'ry...
VERSE 3
Don't let the light go out...
CHORUS

Parts 1 and 2 for B♭ Instruments

Light One Candle

Music: **Peter Yarrow**

Arranged by **Emily Tummons**

Corresponding choral arrangement available in *Kol Han'shamah: Choir Volume II* (TMP 994068)

25
30
Light one candle...
VERSE 2
mp
36
mf
42
48
Don't let the light go out...
CHORUS
f

What is the mem'ry...
VERSE 3
Don't let the light go out...
CHORUS

Parts 1 and 2 for E♭ Instruments

Light One Candle

Music: **Peter Yarrow**

Arranged by **Emily Tummons**

Corresponding choral arrangement available in *Kol Han'shamah: Choir Volume II* (TMP 994068)

25
1
2
30
Light one candle...
VERSE 2
mp
36
mp
mf
42
48
Don't let the light go out...
CHORUS
f

What is the mem'ry...
VERSE 3
mp
mf
f
Don't let the light go out...
CHORUS

80
1
2
84
1
2

Bass

Light One Candle

Music: **Peter Yarrow**

Arranged by **Emily Tummons**

Corresponding choral arrangement available in *Kol Han'shamah: Choir Volume II* (TMP 994068)

Fm Fm/Eb Db Ab/C Bb Ab Fm Ab Fm
CHORUS Don't let the light go out...
Db Eb7 Ab C7 F7 Bbm Eb7 Ab C7
F7 Bbm Eb7 Ab C Fm
VERSE 3 What is the mem'ry...
Ab Ab/G Fm Fm/Eb Db
C7 Fm Fm/Eb Db Ab/C Bb Ab Fm
CHORUS Don't let the light go out...
Ab Fm Db Eb7 Ab C F7 Bbm Eb7
Ab C7 F7 Bbm Eb7 Ab C7
F7 Bbm F7 Bbm F7 Bbm

Full Score

Mi Chamochah

מי כמוכה

Text: **Evening liturgy**

Music: **Dan Nichols** and **Mason Cooper**

Arranged by **Emily Tummons**
Corresponding choral arrangement by **Susan Lewis Friedman**
Piano arrangement by **Susan Lewis Friedman** and **Gregory Shifrin**

Upbeat rock ♩ = 124
Small notes indicate optional solo treble instrument

Corresponding choral arrangement available in *Kol Han'shamah: Choir Volume II* (TMP 994068)

Mel.
1
2
Bass
Pno.
F Gm B♭ C F Gm B♭
Mi cha-mo-chah_ ba-ei-lim,__ A-do-nai! Mi ka-mo-chah_ ne-dar ba-ko-
Lai lai lai lai__ lai lai lai___ lai lai lai lai, lai lai lai lai__ lai lai lai__ lai
E♭ E♭/D C(sus4) C B F Gm B♭ C(sus4)
Last time to Coda
desh.
lai.
No-ra,__ t'-hi-lot,
Last time to Coda

17
F Gm B♭ C F Gm B♭ C(sus4)
Mel.
o - seih___ fe - le!___ No - ra,___ t' - hi - lot,___
1
2
Bass
Pno.
21
F Gm B♭ C(sus4) E♭ Dm
Mel.
o - seih,___ fe - le!___ A - do - nai yim - loch l' - o - lam va -
tr
1
2
Bass
Pno.

25
C(sus4) C C F Gm B♭ C(sus4)
Mel.
ed.___ Mal - chu - t'-cha__ ra - u va - ne - cha, bo -
1
2
Bass
Pno.
29
F Gm B♭ C F Gm B♭ C
Mel.
kei - a yam__ lif - nei Mo - she u - Mir - yam. Zeh Ei - li,__ a - nu__ v'-am' - ru,
1
2
Bass
Pno.

F Gm B♭ C(sus4) E♭
33
Mel.
zeh Ei - li, a - nu v'-am'-ru, A - do - nai yim - loch l'-o-lam va -
1
2
Bass
Pno.
CODA
C(sus4) C
37
D.S. al Coda
ed.
C(sus4) C F
rit.
rit.

Who is like You, O God, among the gods that are worshiped? Who is like You, majestic in holiness, awesome in splendor, working wonders?	מִי־כָמְכָה בָּאֵלִם, יְיָ! מִי כָּמְכָה נֶאְדָּר בַּקֹּדֶשׁ, נוֹרָא תְהִלֹּת, עֹשֵׂה פֶלֶא!
Your children witnessed Your sovereignty, the sea splitting before Moses and Miriam. "This is our God!" they cried. "Adonai will reign forever and ever!"	מַלְכוּתְךָ רָאוּ בָנֶיךָ, בּוֹקֵעַ יָם לִפְנֵי מֹשֶׁה וּמִרְיָם. זֶה אֵלִי, עָנוּ וְאָמְרוּ, יְיָ יִמְלֹךְ לְעוֹלָם וָעֶד!
Thus it is said, "Adonai redeemed Jacob, from a hand stronger than his own." Praised are You, Adonai, for redeeming Israel.	וְנֶאֱמַר: כִּי פָדָה יְיָ אֶת־יַעֲקֹב, וּגְאָלוֹ מִיַּד חָזָק מִמֶּנּוּ. בָּרוּךְ אַתָּה, יְיָ, גָּאַל יִשְׂרָאֵל.

Piano / Vocal

Mi Chamochah

מי כמוכה

Text: **Evening liturgy**

Music: **Dan Nichols** and **Mason Cooper**

Corresponding band arrangement by **Emily Tummons**
Corresponding choral arrangement by **Susan Lewis Friedman**
Piano arrangement by **Susan Lewis Friedman** and **Gregory Shifrin**

Corresponding choral arrangement available in *Kol Han'shamah: Choir Volume II* (TMP 994068)

E♭ E♭/D C(sus4) C
B
F Gm B♭ C(sus4)
Last time to Coda
desh.
lai.
No - ra, t' - hi - lot,
Last time to Coda
F Gm B♭ C F Gm B♭ C(sus4)
o - seih fe - le! No - ra, t' - hi - lot,
F Gm B♭ C(sus4) E♭ Dm
o - seih, fe - le! A - do - nai yim - loch l' - o - lam va -
C(sus4) C
C
F Gm B♭ C(sus4)
ed. Mal - chu - t' - cha ra - u va - ne - cha, bo -

29
F Gm Bb C F Gm Bb C
kei - a yam__ lif - nei Mo - she u - Mir - yam. Zeh Ei - li,__ a - nu__ v'-am' - ru,
33
F Gm Bb C(sus4) Eb
zeh Ei - li,__ a - nu__ v'-am'-ru, A - do - nai yim - loch l' - o - lam va -
CODA
37
C(sus4) C
D.S. al Coda
ed.
C(sus4) C F
rit.

Lead Sheet / Melody for C Instruments

Mi Chamochah

מי כמוכה

Text: **Evening liturgy**

Music: **Dan Nichols** and **Mason Cooper**

Arranged by **Emily Tummons**
Corresponding choral arrangement by **Susan Lewis Friedman**

Corresponding choral arrangement available in *Kol Han'shamah: Choir Volume II* (TMP 994068)

C
D Em G A(sus4) D Em
F Gm B♭ C(sus4) F Gm
chu - t' - cha ra - u va - ne - cha, bo - kei - a yam lif - nei Mo -
G A D Em G A
B♭ C F Gm B♭ C
she u - Mir - yam. Zeh Ei - li, a - nu v' - am' - ru,
D Em G A(sus4) C
F Gm B♭ C(sus4) E♭
zeh Ei - li, a - nu v' - am' - ru, A - do - nai yim - loch l' - o - lam va -
CODA
A(sus4) A
C(sus4) C
D.S. al Coda
ed.
A(sus4) A D
C(sus4) C F
rit.

Melody for B♭ Instruments

Mi Chamochah

מי כמוכה

Music: **Dan Nichols** and **Mason Cooper**

Arranged by **Emily Tummons**

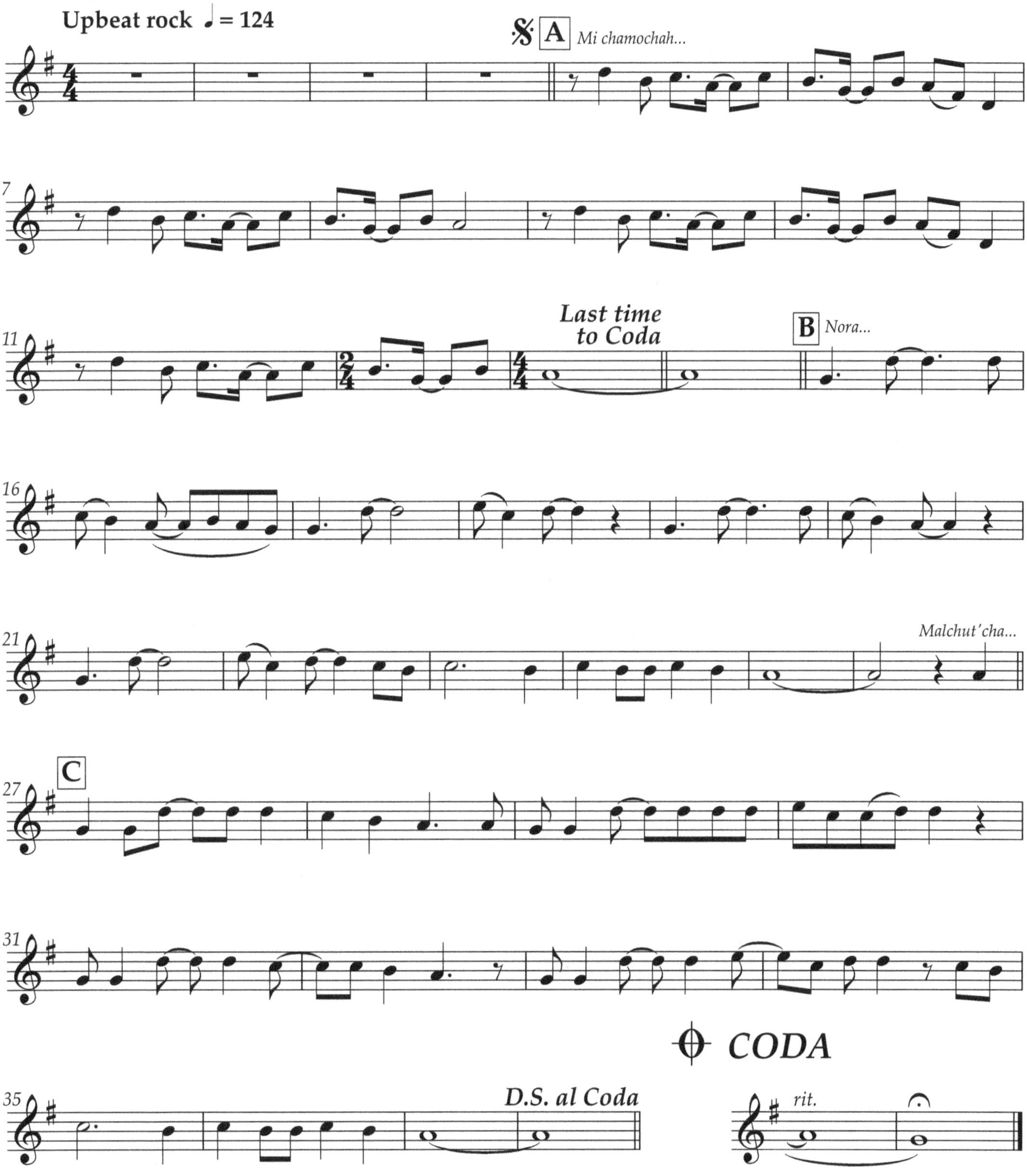

Corresponding choral arrangement available in *Kol Han'shamah: Choir Volume II* (TMP 994068)

Melody for E♭ Instruments

Mi Chamochah

מי כמוכה

Music: **Dan Nichols** and **Mason Cooper**

Arranged by **Emily Tummons**

Corresponding choral arrangement available in *Kol Han'shamah: Choir Volume II* (TMP 994068)

Melody for Bass Clef Instruments

Mi Chamochah

מי כמוכה

Music: **Dan Nichols** and **Mason Cooper**

Arranged by **Emily Tummons**

Corresponding choral arrangement available in *Kol Han'shamah: Choir Volume II* (TMP 994068)

Parts 1 and 2 for C Instruments

Mi Chamochah

מי כמוכה

Music: **Dan Nichols** and **Mason Cooper**

Arranged by **Emily Tummons**

Corresponding choral arrangement available in *Kol Han'shamah: Choir Volume II* (TMP 994068)

C
Malchut'cha...
tr
CODA
D.S. al Coda
rit.
rit.

Parts 1 and 2 for B♭ Instruments

Mi Chamochah

מי כמוכה

Music: **Dan Nichols** and **Mason Cooper**

Arranged by **Emily Tummons**

Corresponding choral arrangement available in *Kol Han'shamah: Choir Volume II* (TMP 994068)

C
Malchut'cha...
CODA
D.S. al Coda
rit.
rit.

Parts 1 and 2 for E♭ Instruments

Mi Chamochah

מי כמוכה

Music: **Dan Nichols** and **Mason Cooper**

Arranged by **Emily Tummons**

Corresponding choral arrangement available in *Kol Han'shamah: Choir Volume II* (TMP 994068)

21
tr
C
Malchut'cha...
26
31
36
D.S. al Coda
CODA
rit.
rit.

Bass

Mi Chamochah

מי כמוכה

Music: **Dan Nichols** and **Mason Cooper**

Arranged by **Emily Tummons**

Corresponding choral arrangement available in *Kol Han'shamah: Choir Volume II* (TMP 994068)

Full Score

Mi Shebeirach

מי שברך

Text: **Debbie Friedman** and **Drorah Setel** (based on liturgy)

Music: **Debbie Friedman**

Arranged by **Emily Tummons**
Corresponding choral arrangement by **Susan Lewis Friedman** and **David Berger**
Piano arrangement by **Alan Mason**

Corresponding choral arrangement available in *Kol Han'shamah: Choir Volume II* (TMP 994068)

7
Am Em F G C Dm7 Em
Mel.
May the Source of strength who blessed the ones be - fore us help us find the cour - age to
1
2
Bass
Pno.

10
Dm Am7 Dm7 G7 C
Mel.
make our lives a bless - ing, and let us say, a - mein.
1
2
Bass
Pno.

B
13
C Am Em F G(sus4) G C Am
Mel.
Mi she - bei - rach i - mo - tei - nu m' - kor ha - b'ra - chah la -
1
2
Bass
Pno.
16
Em7 F G Am Em7 F G C
Mel.
a - vo - tei - nu. Bless those in need of heal - ing with r' - fu - ah sh'lei - mah, the re -
1
2
Bass
Pno.

May the One who blessed our fathers
be the source of blessing for our mothers.
May the One who blessed our mothers
be the source of blessing for our fathers.

מִי שֶׁבֵּרַךְ אֲבוֹתֵינוּ
מְקוֹר הַבְּרָכָה לְאִמּוֹתֵינוּ.
מִי שֶׁבֵּרַךְ אִמּוֹתֵינוּ
מְקוֹר הַבְּרָכָה לַאֲבוֹתֵינוּ.

Piano / Vocal

Mi Shebeirach

מי שברך

Text: **Debbie Friedman** and **Drorah Setel** (based on liturgy)

Music: **Debbie Friedman**

Corresponding band arrangement by **Emily Tummons**
Corresponding choral arrangement by **Susan Lewis Friedman** and **David Berger**
Piano arrangement by **Alan Mason**

Corresponding choral arrangement available in *Kol Han'shamah: Choir Volume II* (TMP 994068)

10
Dm Am7 Dm7 G7 C
make our lives a bless-ing, and let us say, a - mein.
B
13
C Am Em F G(sus4) G C Am
Mi she - bei - rach i - mo - tei - nu m' - kor ha - b'ra - chah la
16
Em7 F G Am Em7 F G C
a - vo - tei - nu. Bless those in need of heal-ing with r' - fu - ah sh'lei - mah, the re-

Dm Em7 Dm Am7 Dm7 G(sus4) G7
19
new - al of bo - dy, the re - new - al of spir - it, and let us say, a -
C Am Em Dm7 G7 C
22
mein, a - mein, a - mein, a - mein.

Lead Sheet / Melody for C Instruments

Mi Shebeirach

מי שברך

Text: **Debbie Friedman** and **Drorah Setel** (based on liturgy)

Music: **Debbie Friedman**

Arranged by **Emily Tummons**
Corresponding choral arrangement by **Susan Lewis Friedman** and **David Berger**

Corresponding choral arrangement available in *Kol Han'shamah: Choir Volume II* (TMP 994068)

Melody for B♭ Instruments

Mi Shebeirach

מי שברך

Music: **Debbie Friedman**

Arranged by **Emily Tummons**

Corresponding choral arrangement available in *Kol Han'shamah: Choir Volume II* (TMP 994068)

Melody for E♭ Instruments

Mi Shebeirach

מי שברך

Music: **Debbie Friedman**

Arranged by **Emily Tummons**

Corresponding choral arrangement available in *Kol Han'shamah: Choir Volume II* (TMP 994068)

Melody for Bass Clef Instruments

Mi Shebeirach

מי שברך

Music: **Debbie Friedman**

Arranged by **Emily Tummons**

Corresponding choral arrangement available in *Kol Han'shamah: Choir Volume II* (TMP 994068)

Parts 1 and 2 for C Instruments

Mi Shebeirach

מי שברך

Music: **Debbie Friedman**

Arranged by **Emily Tummons**

Prayerfully ♩ = 56

Small notes indicate optional solo treble instrument

Corresponding choral arrangement available in *Kol Han'shamah: Choir Volume II* (TMP 994068)

18
1
2
22
1
2

Parts 1 and 2 for B♭ Instruments

Mi Shebeirach

מי שברך

Music: **Debbie Friedman**

Arranged by **Emily Tummons**

Corresponding choral arrangement available in *Kol Han'shamah: Choir Volume II* (TMP 994068)

18
1
2
22
1
2

Parts 1 and 2 for E♭ Instruments

Mi Shebeirach

מי שברך

Music: **Debbie Friedman**

Arranged by **Emily Tummons**

Corresponding choral arrangement available in *Kol Han'shamah: Choir Volume II* (TMP 994068)

18
1
2
22
1
2

Bass

Mi Shebeirach

מי שברך

Music: **Debbie Friedman**

Arranged by **Emily Tummons**

Corresponding choral arrangement available in *Kol Han'shamah: Choir Volume II* (TMP 994068)

Full Score

Olam Chesed Yibaneh

עולם חסד יבנה

Hebrew text: **Psalm 89:3**

Music and English text: **Menachem Creditor**

Arranged by **Emily Tummons**
Piano arrangement and corresponding choral arrangement
by **Rachelle Nelson**

Corresponding choral arrangement available in *Kol Han'shamah: Choir Volume II* (TMP 994068)

D♭maj7 E♭(add9) Fm E♭
Mel.
oo oo
1
2
Bass
Pno.
D♭maj7 E♭(add9) Fm B Fm E♭(add9) D♭ E♭
O - lam che-sed yi-ba - neh, ya la lai lai lai lai

Fm
E♭(add9)
D♭
E♭
Fm
Mel.
lai. O - lam che-sed yi-ba - neh, ya-la - lai lai lai lai lai.
1
2
Bass
Pno.
C
A♭
E♭(add9)
D♭
E♭
Fm
A♭
O - lam che-sed yi-ba - neh, ya la lai lai lai lai lai. O - lam che-sed yi-ba-
mp
mp

28
Mel.
1
2
Bass
Pno.
E♭(add9) E♭ D♭ E♭ Fm D Fm
neh, ya la lai lai lai lai lai lai.
I will build this world from
32
E♭(add9) D♭ E♭ Fm
love, ya la lai lai lai lai lai,
and you must build this world from
mp

E♭(add9) D♭ E♭ Fm E A♭
Mel.
love, ya la lai lai lai lai lai. And if we build this world from
1
2
Bass
Pno.
mf
E♭(add9) D♭ E♭ Fm A♭
love, ya la lai lai lai lai lai, then God will build this world from

Mel.
1
2
Bass
Pno.
E♭(add9) D♭ E♭ Fm F Fm
love, ya la lai lai lai lai__ lai lai.
oo
E♭(add9) D♭maj7 E♭(add9) Fm
oo
oo
p
p

Your steadfast love is confirmed forever.

עוֹלָם חֶסֶד יִבָּנֶה.

Piano / Vocal

Olam Chesed Yibaneh

עולם חסד יבנה

Hebrew text: **Psalm 89:3**

Music and English text: **Menachem Creditor**

Corresponding band arrangement by **Emily Tummons**
Piano arrangement and corresponding choral arrangement
by **Rachelle Nelson**

Corresponding choral arrangement available in *Kol Han'shamah: Choir Volume II* (TMP 994068)

D♭maj7 E♭(add9) Fm B Fm E♭(add9)
O - lam che-sed yi - ba - neh, ya la
D♭ E♭ Fm E♭(add9)
lai lai lai lai lai. O - lam che-sed yi - ba - neh, ya-la
D♭ E♭ Fm C A♭ E♭(add9)
lai lai lai lai lai. O - lam che-sed yi - ba - neh, ya la

25
D♭ E♭ Fm A♭ E♭(add9) E♭
lai lai lai lai lai. O - lam che-sed yi - ba - neh, ya la
29
D♭ E♭ Fm
D
Fm
lai lai lai lai lai lai. I will build this world from
32
E♭(add9) D♭ E♭ Fm
love, ya la lai lai lai lai lai, and you must build this world from

E♭(add9) D♭ E♭ Fm
love, ya la lai lai lai lai lai.
And
E A♭ E♭(add9) D♭ E♭
if we build this world from love, ya la lai lai lai lai
Fm A♭ E♭(add9)
lai, then God will build this world from love, ya la

D♭ E♭ Fm F Fm E♭(add9)
lai lai lai lai lai lai.
oo
oo
D♭maj7 E♭(add9) Fm E♭
oo
ya la
D♭maj7 E♭(add9) Fm
rit.
lai lai lai lai lai lai.
rit.

Lead Sheet / Melody for C Instruments

Olam Chesed Yibaneh

עולם חסד יבנה

Hebrew text: **Psalm 89:3**

Music and English text: **Menachem Creditor**

Arranged by **Emily Tummons**

Corresponding choral arrangement by **Rachelle Nelson**

Corresponding choral arrangement available in *Kol Han'shamah: Choir Volume II* (TMP 994068)

38
Em Fm
E
G A♭
D(add9) E♭(add9)
C D♭
D E♭
lai. And if we build this world from love, ya la lai lai lai lai
42
Em Fm
G A♭
D(add9) E♭(add9)
C D♭
D E♭
lai, then God will build this world from love, ya la lai lai lai lai lai
46
Em Fm
F
Em Fm
D(add9) E♭(add9)
Cmaj7 D♭maj7
D(add9) E♭(add9)
Em Fm
lai. oo oo
51
D E♭
Cmaj7 D♭maj7
D(add9) E♭(add9)
rit.
Em Fm
oo ya la lai lai lai lai lai lai.

Melody for B♭ Instruments

Olam Chesed Yibaneh

עולם חסד יבנה

Music: **Menachem Creditor**

Arranged by **Emily Tummons**

Corresponding choral arrangement available in *Kol Han'shamah: Choir Volume II* (TMP 994068)

E
38
And if we build...
43
F
oo...
47
51
rit.

Melody for E♭ Instruments

Olam Chesed Yibaneh

עולם חסד יבנה

Music: **Menachem Creditor**

Arranged by **Emily Tummons**

Corresponding choral arrangement available in *Kol Han'shamah: Choir Volume II* (TMP 994068)

38
And if we build...
E
43
47
F
oo...
51
rit.

Melody for Bass Clef Instruments

Olam Chesed Yibaneh

עולם חסד יבנה

Music: **Menachem Creditor**

Arranged by **Emily Tummons**

Corresponding choral arrangement available in *Kol Han'shamah: Choir Volume II* (TMP 994068)

38
E
And if we build...
43
47
F
oo...
51
rit.

Parts 1 and 2 for C Instruments

Olam Chesed Yibaneh

עולם חסד יבנה

Music: **Menachem Creditor**

Arranged by **Emily Tummons**

Corresponding choral arrangement available in *Kol Han'shamah: Choir Volume II* (TMP 994068)

22
C Olam chesed...
mp
26
31
D I will build...
mp
35
And if we build...
39
E mf
mf

43
1
2
47
F
oo...
p
p
52
rit.
rit.

Parts 1 and 2 for B♭ Instruments

Olam Chesed Yibaneh

עולם חסד יבנה

Music: **Menachem Creditor**

Arranged by **Emily Tummons**

Corresponding choral arrangement available in *Kol Han'shamah: Choir Volume II* (TMP 994068)

C
Olam chesed...
D
I will build...
And if we build...
E

43
1
2
47
F
oo...
p
p
52
rit.
rit.

Parts 1 and 2 for E♭ Instruments

Olam Chesed Yibaneh

עולם חסד יבנה

Music: **Menachem Creditor**

Arranged by **Emily Tummons**

Corresponding choral arrangement available in *Kol Han'shamah: Choir Volume II* (TMP 994068)

C
Olam chesed...
D
I will build...
And if we build...
E

43
1
2
47
F
oo...
p
p
52
rit.
rit.

Bass

Olam Chesed Yibaneh

עולם חסד יבנה

Music: **Menachem Creditor**

Arranged by **Emily Tummons**

Starkly, quietly ♩ = 88

Small notes indicate optional solo treble instrument

Corresponding choral arrangement available in *Kol Han'shamah: Choir Volume II* (TMP 994068)

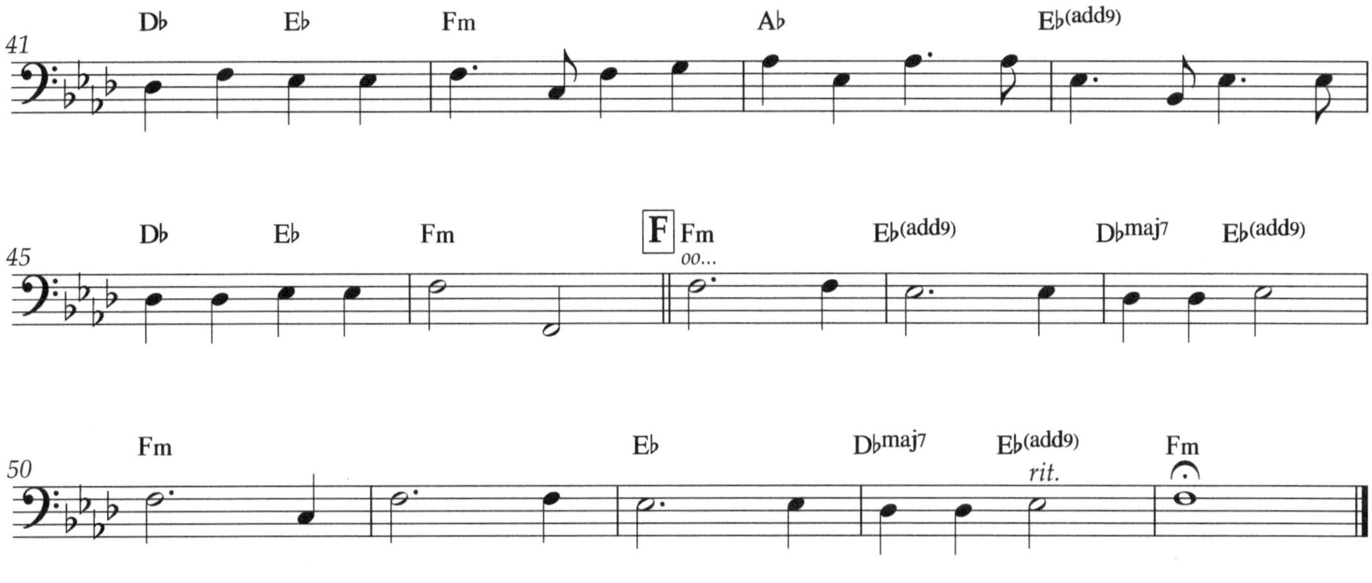
41
D♭ E♭ Fm A♭ E♭(add9)
45
D♭ E♭ Fm
F
Fm
oo...
E♭(add9) D♭maj7 E♭(add9)
50
Fm E♭ D♭maj7 E♭(add9)
rit.
Fm

Full Score

Oseh Shalom

עושה שלום

Text: **Liturgy**

Music and English text: **Elana Jagoda**

Arranged by **Emily Tummons**
Piano arranged by **Susan Lewis Friedman** and **Gregory Shifrin**
Corresponding choral arrangement by **Susan Lewis Friedman**

Corresponding choral arrangement available in *Kol Han'shamah: Choir Volume II* (TMP 994068)

9
Mel.
1
2
Bass
Pno.
A♭
E♭
E♭/D
Cm7
B♭
o - seh sha - lom
bim - - ro - mav,
12
E♭
E♭/D
B
Cm
A♭(add9)
hu ya - a - seh,
hu ya - a - seh,
hu ya - a - seh
mf
mf

14
Eb Bb Cm Ab(add9)
Mel.
shalom, hu ya-a-seh, hu ya-a-seh, hu ya-a-seh
1
2
Bass
Pno.
16
Eb Bb Cm Ab(add9)
Mel.
shalom, hu ya-a-seh, hu ya-a-seh, hu ya-a-seh
1
2
Bass
Pno.

E♭ B♭ B♭(add9)
18
Mel.
— sha-lom a - lei - nu.
mf
1
2
Bass
8va
Pno.
C A♭maj7 B♭ Cm A♭(add9)
1. D.S.
2. Continue
21
May the One, may the One who makes peace bring peace down, bring peace down.—
f
1. D.S.
2. Continue

D
23
Mel.
1
2
Bass
Pno.
A♭maj7 B♭ Cm A♭(add9)
May the One, may the One who makes peace bring peace down, bring peace down.
25
A♭maj7 B♭
Repeat as desired
Cm A♭(add9)
ad lib.
May the One, may the One who makes peace bring peace down, bring peace down.
ad lib.

May the One who makes peace in the high heavens
make peace for us.

עֹשֶׂה שָׁלוֹם בִּמְרוֹמָיו,
הוּא יַעֲשֶׂה שָׁלוֹם עָלֵינוּ.

Piano / Vocal

Oseh Shalom

עושה שלום

Text: **Liturgy**

Music and English text: **Elana Jagoda**

Corresponding band arrangement by **Emily Tummons**
Piano arranged by **Susan Lewis Friedman** and **Gregory Shifrin**
Corresponding choral arrangement by **Susan Lewis Friedman**

Corresponding choral arrangement available in *Kol Han'shamah: Choir Volume II* (TMP 994068)

E♭ E♭/D B Cm A♭(add9)
hu ya - a - seh, hu ya - a - seh, hu ya - a - seh
E♭ B♭ Cm A♭(add9)
sha - lom, hu ya - a - seh, hu ya - a - seh, hu ya - a - seh
E♭ B♭ Cm A♭(add9)
sha - lom, hu ya - a - seh, hu ya - a - seh, hu ya - a - seh

18
E♭
B♭
B♭(add9)
— sha-lom a - lei - nu.
8va
C
21
A♭maj7
B♭
Cm
A♭(add9)
1. D.S.
2. Continue
May the One, may the One who makes peace bring peace down, bring peace down.—
1. D.S.
2. Continue
D
23
A♭maj7
B♭
Cm
A♭(add9)
May the One, may the One who makes peace bring peace down, bring peace down.—

25
Abmaj7
Bb
Repeat as desired
Cm
Ab(add9)
ad lib.
May the One, may the One who makes peace bring peace down, bring peace down.
ad lib.
27
Bb/Eb Eb
Bb/Eb
Eb
Eb(add9)
rit.
Eb(add9)/Bb
Bb(add9)
peace down, bring peace down. a - lei - nu.
rit.

Lead Sheet / Melody for C Instruments

Oseh Shalom

עושה שלום

Text: **Liturgy**

Music and English text: **Elana Jagoda**

Arranged by **Emily Tummons**
Corresponding choral arrangement by **Susan Lewis Friedman**

Corresponding choral arrangement available in *Kol Han'shamah: Choir Volume II* (TMP 994068)

C
Fmaj7 G Am F(add9)
Abmaj7 Bb Cm Ab(add9)
1. D.S.
2. Continue
21
May the One, may the One who makes peace bring peace down, bring peace down.
D
Fmaj7 G Am F(add9)
Abmaj7 Bb Cm Ab(add9)
23
May the One, may the One who makes peace bring peace down, bring peace down.
Repeat as desired
Fmaj7 G Am F(add9)
Abmaj7 Bb Cm Ab(add9)
25
ad lib.
May the One, may the One who makes peace bring peace down, bring peace down.
G/C C G/C C C(add9) C(add9)/G G(add9)
Bb/Eb Eb Bb/Eb Eb Eb(add9) Eb(add9)/Bb Bb(add9)
27
rit.
peace down, bring peace down. a - lei - nu.

Melody for B♭ Instruments

Oseh Shalom

עושה שלום

Music: **Elana Jagoda**

Arranged by **Emily Tummons**

Corresponding choral arrangement available in *Kol Han'shamah: Choir Volume II* (TMP 994068)

Melody for E♭ Instruments

Oseh Shalom

עושה שלום

Music: **Elana Jagoda**

Arranged by **Emily Tummons**

Corresponding choral arrangement available in *Kol Han'shamah: Choir Volume II* (TMP 994068)

Melody for Bass Clef Instruments

Oseh Shalom

עושה שלום

Music: **Elana Jagoda**

Arranged by **Emily Tummons**

Corresponding choral arrangement available in *Kol Han'shamah: Choir Volume II* (TMP 994068)

Parts 1 and 2 for C Instruments

Oseh Shalom

עושה שלום

Music: **Elana Jagoda**

Arranged by **Emily Tummons**

Corresponding choral arrangement available in *Kol Han'shamah: Choir Volume II* (TMP 994068)

23
D
May the One...
1
2
26
Repeat as desired
ad lib.
mf
rit.

Parts 1 and 2 for B♭ Instruments

Oseh Shalom

עושה שלום

Music: **Elana Jagoda**

Arranged by **Emily Tummons**

Corresponding choral arrangement available in *Kol Han'shamah: Choir Volume II* (TMP 994068)

D
May the One...
23
1
2
26
Repeat as desired
mf
rit.

Parts 1 and 2 for E♭ Instruments

Oseh Shalom

עושה שלום

Music: **Elana Jagoda**

Arranged by **Emily Tummons**

Happily, with bold rhythm ♩ = 100

Small notes indicate optional solo treble instrument

Corresponding choral arrangement available in *Kol Han'shamah: Choir Volume II* (TMP 994068)

D
May the One...
23
1
2
26
Repeat as desired
ad lib.
mf
mf
mf
rit.
rit.

Bass

Oseh Shalom

עושה שלום

Music: **Elana Jagoda**

Arranged by **Emily Tummons**

Corresponding choral arrangement available in *Kol Han'shamah: Choir Volume II* (TMP 994068)

Full Score

Shalom Aleichem

שלום עליכם

Text: **Liturgy**

Music: **Sol Zim**

Arranged by **Emily Tummons**
Piano arrangement and corresponding choral arrangement
by **Robbie Solomon**

Corresponding choral arrangement available in *Kol Han'shamah: Choir Volume II* (TMP 994068)

VERSES
Am7 B7 Em B7 Em
Mel.
lai lai lai, lai lai lai lai. 1. Sha - lom a - lei - chem, mal - a - chei ha - sha - reit,
2. Bar' - chu - ni l'-sha - lom, mal - a - chei ha - sha - lom,
solo instrument tacet first time
Verse 1: Parts I & II, tacet until m.21
mf
1
2
Bass
Pno.
Am6 B7
mal - a - chei el - yon, mi - me - lech, mi me - lech mal - chei ham'- la - chim, Ha-
mal - a - chei el - yon, mi - me - lech, mi me - lech mal - chei ham'- la - chim, Ha-

Cmaj7 D7(sus4) D7 G B7 Em
Mel.
Ka - dosh, ba - ruch hu. Bo-a-chem l'-sha-lom, mal-a-chei ha-sha-lom,
Ka - dosh, ba - ruch hu. Tzeit-chem l'-sha-lom, mal-a-chei ha-sha-lom,
mf
1
2
Bass
Pno.
Am6 B7
mal - a - chei el - yon, mi - me - lech, mi - me - lech
mal - a - chei el - yon, mi - me - lech, mi - me - lech

Em E7 1. D.S.
2. D.S. al Coda
Mel.
mal-chei ham'-la-chim, Ha - Ka - dosh, ba - ruch hu.
mal-chei ham'-la-chim, Ha - Ka - dosh, ba - ruch hu.
Yai lai lai
1
2
Bass
Pno.
CODA
Am7 B7 Em B7 Em
non-rit.
lai lai lai, lai lai lai lai.
non-rit.

Peace be to you, O ministering angels,
messengers of the Most High,
Majesty of majesties,
Holy One of Blessing.

Enter in peace, O messengers of peace,
angels of the Most High,
Majesty of majesties,
Holy One of Blessing.

Bless me with peace, O messengers of peace,
angels of the Most High,
Majesty of majesties,
Holy One of Blessing.

Depart in peace, O messengers of peace,
angels of the Most High,
Majesty of majesties,
Holy One of Blessing.

שָׁלוֹם עֲלֵיכֶם, מַלְאֲכֵי הַשָּׁרֵת,
מַלְאֲכֵי עֶלְיוֹן,
מִמֶּלֶךְ מַלְכֵי הַמְּלָכִים,
הַקָּדוֹשׁ בָּרוּךְ הוּא.

בּוֹאֲכֶם לְשָׁלוֹם, מַלְאֲכֵי הַשָּׁלוֹם,
מַלְאֲכֵי עֶלְיוֹן,
מִמֶּלֶךְ מַלְכֵי הַמְּלָכִים,
הַקָּדוֹשׁ בָּרוּךְ הוּא.

בָּרְכוּנִי לְשָׁלוֹם, מַלְאֲכֵי הַשָּׁלוֹם,
מַלְאֲכֵי עֶלְיוֹן,
מִמֶּלֶךְ מַלְכֵי הַמְּלָכִים,
הַקָּדוֹשׁ בָּרוּךְ הוּא.

צֵאתְכֶם לְשָׁלוֹם, מַלְאֲכֵי הַשָּׁלוֹם,
מַלְאֲכֵי עֶלְיוֹן,
מִמֶּלֶךְ מַלְכֵי הַמְּלָכִים,
הַקָּדוֹשׁ בָּרוּךְ הוּא.

Piano / Vocal

Shalom Aleichem

שלום עליכם

Text: **Liturgy**

Music: **Sol Zim**

Corresponding band arrangement by **Emily Tummons**
Piano arrangement and corresponding choral arrangement by **Robbie Solomon**

Corresponding choral arrangement available in *Kol Han'shamah: Choir Volume II* (TMP 994068)

Am6 B7
mal-a-chei el - yon, mi - me- lech, mi me-lech mal-chei ham'-la-chim, Ha
mal-a-chei el - yon, mi - me- lech, mi me-lech mal-chei ham'-la-chim, Ha
Cmaj7 D7(sus4) D7 G B7 Em
Ka - dosh, ba - ruch hu. Bo-a-chem l' sha-lom, mal-a-chei ha-sha-lom,
Ka - dosh, ba - ruch hu. Tzeit-chem l' sha-lom, mal-a-chei ha-sha-lom,
Am6 B7
mal-a-chei el - yon, mi - me- lech, mi-me-lech mal-chei ham'-la-chim, Ha
mal-a-chei el - yon, mi - me- lech, mi-me-lech mal-chei ham'-la-chim, Ha
CODA
Em E7 1. D.S. 2. D.S. al Coda
Ka-dosh, ba-ruch hu.
Ka-dosh, ba-ruch hu.
Yai lai lai
Am7 B7 Em B7 Em
non-rit.
lai lai lai, lai lai lai lai.

Lead Sheet / Melody for C Instruments

Shalom Aleichem

שלום עליכם

Text: **Liturgy**

Music: **Sol Zim**

Arranged by **Emily Tummons**
Corresponding choral arrangement by **Robbie Solomon**

Corresponding choral arrangement available in *Kol Han'shamah: Choir Volume II* (TMP 994068)

Melody for B♭ Instruments

Shalom Aleichem

שלום עליכם

Music: **Sol Zim**

Arranged by **Emily Tummons**

Corresponding choral arrangement available in *Kol Han'shamah: Choir Volume II* (TMP 994068)

Melody for E♭ Instruments

Shalom Aleichem

שלום עליכם

Music: **Sol Zim**

Arranged by **Emily Tummons**

Corresponding choral arrangement available in *Kol Han'shamah: Choir Volume II* (TMP 994068)

Melody for Bass Clef Instruments

Shalom Aleichem

שלום עליכם

Music: **Sol Zim**

Arranged by **Emily Tummons**

Corresponding choral arrangement available in *Kol Han'shamah: Choir Volume II* (TMP 994068)

Parts 1 and 2 for C Instruments

Shalom Aleichem

שלום עליכם

Music: **Sol Zim**

Arranged by **Emily Tummons**

Strongly; Chasidic style ♩ = 100

Small notes indicate optional solo treble instrument

Corresponding choral arrangement available in *Kol Han'shamah: Choir Volume II* (TMP 994068)

17
mf
mf
mf
20
24
tr
1. D.S.
2. D.S. al Coda
f
f
CODA
27
non-rit.
non-rit.

Parts 1 and 2 for B♭ Instruments

Shalom Aleichem

שלום עליכם

Music: **Sol Zim**

Arranged by **Emily Tummons**

Corresponding choral arrangement available in *Kol Han'shamah: Choir Volume II* (TMP 994068)

17
mf
20
24
tr
1. D.S.
2. D.S. al Coda
f
CODA
27
non-rit.

Parts 1 and 2 for E♭ Instruments

Shalom Aleichem

שלום עליכם

Music: **Sol Zim**

Arranged by **Emily Tummons**

Corresponding choral arrangement available in *Kol Han'shamah: Choir Volume II* (TMP 994068)

mf
tr
1. D.S.
2. D.S. al Coda
f
CODA
non-rit.

Bass

Shalom Aleichem

שלום עליכם

Music: **Sol Zim**

Arranged by **Emily Tummons**

Corresponding choral arrangement available in *Kol Han'shamah: Choir Volume II* (TMP 994068)

Full Score

Shalom Rav

שלום רב

Text: **Evening liturgy**

Music: **Jeff Klepper** and **Dan Freelander**

Arranged by **Emily Tummons**
Piano arranged by **Rachelle Nelson** and **Gregory Shifrin**
Corresponding choral arrangement by **Rachelle Nelson**

Pop feel; with movement ♩ = 88
Small notes indicate optional solo treble instrument

Corresponding choral arrangement available in *Kol Han'shamah: Choir Volume II* (TMP 994068)

A
9
D(add9) C(add9)/D G/D A/D
Mel.
rav al Yis-ra-el am'-cha ta-sim l'-o-lam. Sha-lom
1
2
p
Bass
Pno.
13
D(add9) C(add9)/D G/D A/D D
rav al Yis-ra-el am'-cha ta-sim l'-o-lam.

B
17
A
G(add9)
A(sus4)
A
G
Mel.
Ki a-tah hu Me-lech A-don l'-chol ha - sha-lom,
1
2
mp
Bass
Pno.
21
A
G(add9)
Em7
A(sus4)
A
ki a-tah hu Me-lech A-don l'-chol ha - sha - lom. Sha-lom
mf

C
D(add9) C(add9)/D G/D A/D
Mel.
rav al Yis-ra-el am'-cha ta-sim l'-o-lam, sha-lom
1
2
Bass
Pno.
mf
D(add9) C(add9)/D G/D A/D D
rav al Yis-ra-el am'-cha ta-sim l'-o-lam. V'-
mp

D
33
Em C D D/C# Bm Bm/A Em A(sus4) A D F#(sus4) F#7
Mel.
tov b'-ei-ne-cha l'-va-reich__ et am'-cha__ Yis-ra-el
1
2
Bass
Pno.
mp
37
Em F#7 Bm Bm/A Em G/A G A(sus4)
b'-chol eit__ u-v-chol sha-ah__ bish-lo-me-cha.__ Sha-lom
mf

E
D(add9)
C(add9)/D
G/D
A/D
41
Mel.
rav al Yis-ra-el am'-cha ta-sim l'-o-lam, sha-lom
1
mf
2
mf
Bass
Pno.
D(add9)
C(add9)/D
G/D
A/D
D
45
Mel.
rav al Yis-ra-el am'-cha ta-sim l'-o-lam, ta-
1
2
Bass
Pno.

Grant abundant peace to Israel
Your people forever,
for You are the Sovereign God
of all peace.
May it be pleasing to You
to bless Your people Israel
in every season and moment with Your peace.

שָׁלוֹם רָב עַל יִשְׂרָאֵל עַמְּךָ
תָּשִׂים לְעוֹלָם,
כִּי אַתָּה הוּא מֶלֶךְ אָדוֹן
לְכָל הַשָּׁלוֹם.
וְטוֹב בְּעֵינֶיךָ לְבָרֵךְ
אֶת עַמְּךָ יִשְׂרָאֵל
בְּכָל עֵת וּבְכָל שָׁעָה בִּשְׁלוֹמֶךָ.

Piano / Vocal

Shalom Rav

שלום רב

Text: **Evening liturgy**

Music: **Jeff Klepper** and **Dan Freelander**

Corresponding band arrangement by **Emily Tummons**
Piano arranged by **Rachelle Nelson** and **Gregory Shifrin**
Corresponding choral arrangement by **Rachelle Nelson**

Corresponding choral arrangement available in *Kol Han'shamah: Choir Volume II* (TMP 994068)

D(add9) C(add9)/D G/D A/D D
rav al Yis-ra - el am' - cha ta - sim l' - o - lam.
B
A G(add9) A(sus4) A G
Ki a-tah hu Me-lech A-don l'-chol ha - sha-lom,
A G(add9) Em7 A(sus4) A
ki a-tah hu Me-lech A-don l'-chol ha - sha - lom. Sha-lom

C
D(add9) C(add9)/D G/D A/D
25
rav al Yis-ra - el am' - cha ta - sim l' - o - lam, sha-lom
D(add9) C(add9)/D G/D A/D D
29
rav al Yis-ra - el am' - cha ta - sim l' - o - lam. V'-
D
Em C D D/C♯ Bm Bm/A Em A(sus4) A D F♯(sus4) F♯7
33
tov b' - ei - ne - cha l' - va - reich et am' - cha Yis - ra - el

37
Em F#7 Bm Bm/A Em G/A G A(sus4)
b' - chol eit u - v - chol sha-ah bish - lo - me - cha. Sha-lom
E
41
D(add9) C(add9)/D G/D A/D
rav al Yis-ra - el am' - cha ta - sim l' - o - lam, sha-lom
45
D(add9) C(add9)/D G/D A/D D
rav al Yis-ra - el am' - cha ta - sim l' - o - lam, ta-
49
G/D A/D D C/D D
sim l' - o - lam, ta - sim l' - o - lam.

Lead Sheet / Melody for C Instruments

Shalom Rav

שלום רב

Text: **Evening liturgy**

Music: **Jeff Klepper** and **Dan Freelander**

Arranged by **Emily Tummons**
Corresponding choral arrangement by **Rachelle Nelson**

Corresponding choral arrangement available in *Kol Han'shamah: Choir Volume II* (TMP 994068)

D
33
Em C D D/C♯ Bm Bm/A Em A(sus4) A D F♯(sus4) F♯7
tov b' - ei - ne - cha l' - va - reich et am' - cha Yis - ra - el
37
Em F♯7 Bm Bm/A Em G/A G A(sus4)
b' - chol eit u - v - chol sha - ah bish - lo - me - cha. Sha - lom
E
41
D(add9) C(add9)/D G/D A/D
rav al Yis - ra - el am' - cha ta - sim l' - o - lam, sha - lom
45
D(add9) C(add9)/D G/D A/D D
rav al Yis - ra - el am' - cha ta - sim l' - o - lam, ta -
49
G/D A/D D C/D D
sim l' - o - lam, ta - sim l' - o - lam.

Melody for B♭ Instruments

Shalom Rav

שלום רב

Music: **Jeff Klepper** and **Dan Freelander**

Arranged by **Emily Tummons**

Corresponding choral arrangement available in *Kol Han'shamah: Choir Volume II* (TMP 994068)

D
33
37
Shalom rav...
E
41
45
49

Melody for E♭ Instruments

Shalom Rav

שלום רב

Music: **Jeff Klepper** and **Dan Freelander**

Arranged by **Emily Tummons**

Corresponding choral arrangement available in *Kol Han'shamah: Choir Volume II* (TMP 994068)

D
E
Shalom rav...

Melody for Bass Clef Instruments

Shalom Rav

שלום רב

Music: **Jeff Klepper** and **Dan Freelander**

Arranged by **Emily Tummons**

Pop feel; with movement ♩ = 88

Corresponding choral arrangement available in *Kol Han'shamah: Choir Volume II* (TMP 994068)

D
33
37
Shalom rav...
E
41
45
49

Parts 1 and 2 for C Instruments

Shalom Rav

שלום רב

Music: **Jeff Klepper** and **Dan Freelander**

Arranged by **Emily Tummons**

Corresponding choral arrangement available in *Kol Han'shamah: Choir Volume II* (TMP 994068)

Shalom rav...
C
V'tov...
D
mf
mp

Shalom rav...
E
40
44
48
1
2
mf
mp

Parts 1 and 2 for B♭ Instruments

Shalom Rav

שלום רב

Music: **Jeff Klepper** and **Dan Freelander**

Arranged by **Emily Tummons**

Corresponding choral arrangement available in *Kol Han'shamah: Choir Volume II* (TMP 994068)

20
1
2
24
Shalom rav...
C
mf
28
32
V'tov...
D
mp
36

Shalom rav...
E
mf
mp

Parts 1 and 2 for E♭ Instruments

Shalom Rav

שלום רב

Music: **Jeff Klepper** and **Dan Freelander**

Arranged by **Emily Tummons**

Pop feel; with movement ♩ = 88

Small notes indicate optional solo treble instrument

Corresponding choral arrangement available in *Kol Han'shamah: Choir Volume II* (TMP 994068)

20
1
2
24
Shalom rav...
C
mf
28
32
V'tov...
D
mp
36

Shalom rav...
E
mf
mp

Bass

Shalom Rav

שלום רב

Music: **Jeff Klepper** and **Dan Freelander**

Arranged by **Emily Tummons**

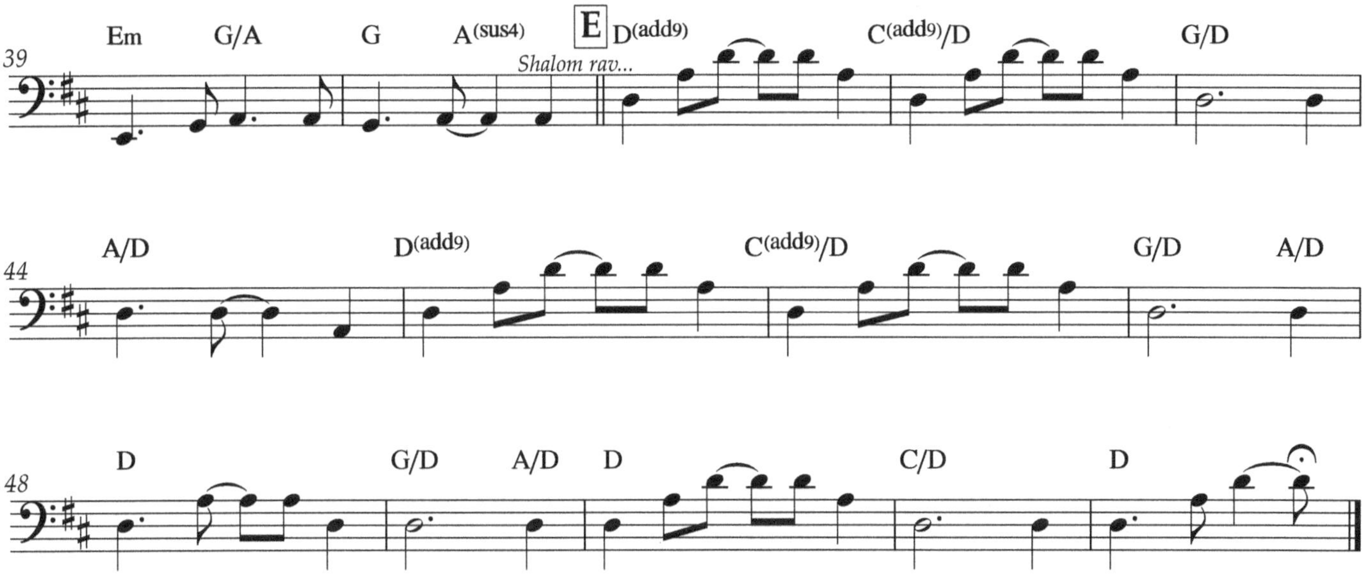
39
Em G/A G A(sus4)
E
D(add9)
Shalom rav...
C(add9)/D G/D
44
A/D D(add9) C(add9)/D G/D A/D
48
D G/D A/D D C/D D

Full Score

Shir Chadash

שיר חדש

Hebrew text: **Based on Psalm 96:1**

Music and English Text: **Julie Silver**

Arranged by **Emily Tummons**
Piano arrangement and corresponding choral arrangement
by **Robbie Solomon**

Corresponding choral arrangement available in *Kol Han'shamah: Choir Volume II* (TMP 994068)

17
Dm7
G
Last time to Coda
1. C(sus4)
G
2. C(sus4)
C
B
B♭
Mel.
shir cha - dash.
dash.
Sing un - to
1
2
f
f
Bass
Pno.
24
F
C(sus4) C
B♭
F
C
God, all the earth, a new song. I will sing un - to God a new song.

31
B♭ F C(sus4) C B♭ F
Mel.
Sing un - to God and we'll all sing a - long, all the earth, a new song, un - to
f
1
2
Bass
Pno.
37
G7(sus4) G7 Dm7 G7
D.S. al Coda
God.
D.S. al Coda

CODA

Sing unto God a new song,
sing unto God, all the earth.

שִׁירוּ לַייָ כָּל הָאָרֶץ,
שִׁירוּ לַייָ שִׁיר חָדָשׁ.

Piano / Vocal

Shir Chadash

שיר חדש

Hebrew text: **Based on Psalm 96:1**

Music and English Text: **Julie Silver**

Corresponding band arrangement by **Emily Tummons**
Piano arrangement and corresponding choral arrangement by **Robbie Solomon**

Corresponding choral arrangement available in *Kol Han'shamah: Choir Volume II* (TMP 994068)

2. C(sus4)
C
B
B♭
F
C(sus4) C
dash.
Sing un - to God, all the earth, a new song. I will
sing un - to God a new song.
Sing un - to God and we'll all sing a-long,
all the earth, a new song, un - to God.
G7(sus4)
G7
Dm7
D.S. al Coda
CODA
C(add9)
molto rit.
dash. I will sing un - to God a new song.

Lead Sheet / Melody for C Instruments

Shir Chadash

שיר חדש

Hebrew text: **Based on Psalm 96:1**

Music and English Text: **Julie Silver**

Arranged by **Emily Tummons**
Corresponding choral arrangement by **Robbie Solomon**

Corresponding choral arrangement available in *Kol Han'shamah: Choir Volume II* (TMP 994068)

Melody for B♭ Instruments

Shir Chadash

שיר חדש

Music: **Julie Silver**

Arranged by **Emily Tummons**

Corresponding choral arrangement available in *Kol Han'shamah: Choir Volume II* (TMP 994068)

Melody for E♭ Instruments

Shir Chadash

שיר חדש

Music: **Julie Silver**

Arranged by **Emily Tummons**

Corresponding choral arrangement available in *Kol Han'shamah: Choir Volume II* (TMP 994068)

Melody for Bass Clef Instruments

Shir Chadash

שיר חדש

Music: **Julie Silver**

Arranged by **Emily Tummons**

Parts 1 and 2 for C Instruments

Shir Chadash

שיר חדש

Music: **Julie Silver**

Arranged by **Emily Tummons**

Corresponding choral arrangement available in *Kol Han'shamah: Choir Volume II* (TMP 994068)

f
D.S. al Coda
CODA
molto rit.
molto rit.

Parts 1 and 2 for B♭ Instruments

Shir Chadash

שיר חדש

Music: **Julie Silver**

Arranged by **Emily Tummons**

Corresponding choral arrangement available in *Kol Han'shamah: Choir Volume II* (TMP 994068)

D.S. al Coda
CODA
molto rit.
molto rit.

Parts 1 and 2 for E♭ Instruments

Shir Chadash

שיר חדש

Music: **Julie Silver**

Arranged by **Emily Tummons**

Corresponding choral arrangement available in *Kol Han'shamah: Choir Volume II* (TMP 994068)

f
D.S. al Coda
CODA
molto rit.
molto rit.

Bass

Shir Chadash

שיר חדש

Music: **Julie Silver**

Arranged by **Emily Tummons**

Corresponding choral arrangement available in *Kol Han'shamah: Choir Volume II* (TMP 994068)

Full Score

Y'did Nefesh

ידיד נפש

Text: **Eleazar ben Moses Azikri**

Music: **Ehud** and **Sarah Zweig**

Arranged by **Emily Tummons**
Piano arrangement and corresponding choral arrangement
by **Robbie Solomon**

Corresponding choral arrangement available in *Kol Han'shamah: Choir Volume II* (TMP 994068)

Am B7 Em Em7/D Am D7 G E7
Mel.
m' - shoch av - d' - cha el r' - tzo - ne - cha,
1
2
mp
Bass
Pno.
Am B7 Em Em7 Am B7 Em E7/G#
m' - shoch av - d' - cha d' di di dai dai dai el r' - tzo - ne - cha.

B
33
Am D7 G Cmaj7 Am D7 G Em
Mel.
Ya - rutz av - d' - cha k' - mo a - yal
mf
1
2
Bass
Pno.
41
A/C# B7/D# Em Em7/D Am B7 Em
yish - ta - cha - veh ai d' di di dai dai dai el mul ha - da - re - cha.

48
E7/G♯ C Am D7 G Cmaj7 Am D7
poco a poco accel.
Mel.
Ya - rutz avd'cha k' - mo a -
1
2
Bass
Pno.
poco a poco accel.
55
G E7 Am B7 Cmaj7
yal yish - ta - cha - veh ai d' di di
mp
mp
mp

Heart's delight, Sourcy of mercy, draw Your servant into Your arms. I leap like a deer to stand in awe before You.	יְדִיד נֶפֶשׁ, אָב הָרַחֲמָן, מְשׁוֹךְ עַבְדְּךָ אֶל רְצוֹנֶךָ. יָרוּץ עַבְדְּךָ כְּמוֹ אַיָּל יִשְׁתַּחֲוֶה אֶל מוּל הֲדָרֶךָ.

Piano / Vocal

Y'did Nefesh

ידיד נפש

Text: **Eleazar ben Moses Azikri**

Music: **Ehud** and **Sarah Zweig**

Corresponding band arrangement by **Emily Tummons**
Piano arrangement and corresponding choral arrangement by **Robbie Solomon**

Corresponding choral arrangement available in *Kol Han'shamah: Choir Volume II* (TMP 994068)

23
G E7 Am B7 Em Em7 Am
cha, m' - shoch av - d' - cha d' di di dai dai dai el r' -
30
B7 Em E7/G# B Am D7 G Cmaj7
tzo - ne - cha. Ya - rutz av - d' - cha
37
Am D7 G Em A/C# B7/D# Em
k' - mo a - yal yish - ta - cha - veh ai d' di di

Em7/D Am B7 Em E7/G♯ C Am D7
poco a poco accel.
dai dai dai el mul ha - da - re - cha. Ya - rutz
G Cmaj7 Am D7 G E7 Am
av - d' - cha k' - mo a - yal yish - ta - cha -
B7 Cmaj7 Em7 molto rit. Am B7 Em
veh ai d' di di dai dai dai el mul ha - da - re - cha.

Lead Sheet / Melody for C Instruments

Y'did Nefesh

ידיד נפש

Text: **Eleazar ben Moses Azikri**

Music: **Ehud** and **Sarah Zweig**

Arranged by **Emily Tummons**
Corresponding choral arrangement by **Robbie Solomon**

Melody for B♭ Instruments

Y'did Nefesh

ידיד נפש

Music: **Ehud** and **Sarah Zweig**

Arranged by **Emily Tummons**

Corresponding choral arrangement available in *Kol Han'shamah: Choir Volume II* (TMP 994068)

Melody for E♭ Instruments

Y'did Nefesh

ידיד נפש

Music: **Ehud** and **Sarah Zweig**

Arranged by **Emily Tummons**

Corresponding choral arrangement available in *Kol Han'shamah: Choir Volume II* (TMP 994068)

Melody for Bass Clef Instruments

Y'did Nefesh

ידיד נפש

Music: **Ehud** and **Sarah Zweig**

Arranged by **Emily Tummons**

Corresponding choral arrangement available in *Kol Han'shamah: Choir Volume II* (TMP 994068)

Parts 1 and 2 for C Instruments

Y'did Nefesh

ידיד נפש

Music: **Ehud** and **Sarah Zweig**

Arranged by **Emily Tummons**

Corresponding choral arrangement available in *Kol Han'shamah: Choir Volume II* (TMP 994068)

Yarutz avd'cha...
B
mf
Yarutz avd'cha...
C
poco a poco accel.
poco a poco accel.
mp
molto rit.
molto rit.
mp

Parts 1 and 2 for B♭ Instruments

Y'did Nefesh

ידיד נפש

Music: **Ehud** and **Sarah Zweig**

Arranged by **Emily Tummons**

Corresponding choral arrangement available in *Kol Han'shamah: Choir Volume II* (TMP 994068)

Yarutz avd'cha...
B
mf
33
1
2
mf
mf
40
46
Yarutz avd'cha...
poco a poco accel.
C
poco a poco accel.
52
58
mp
mp
mp
molto rit.
molto rit.

Parts 1 and 2 for E♭ Instruments

Y'did Nefesh

ידיד נפש

Music: **Ehud** and **Sarah Zweig**

Arranged by **Emily Tummons**

Corresponding choral arrangement available in *Kol Han'shamah: Choir Volume II* (TMP 994068)

B
Yarutz avd'cha...
mf
33
40
46
Yarutz avd'cha...
C
poco a poco accel.
poco a poco accel.
52
58
mp
molto rit.
molto rit.

BASS

Y'did Nefesh

ידיד נפש

Music: **Ehud** and **Sarah Zweig**

Arranged by **Emily Tummons**

With a sway ♩ = 124

Corresponding choral arrangement available in *Kol Han'shamah: Choir Volume II* (TMP 994068)

Full Score

Yih'yu L'ratzon

יהיו לרצון

Text: **Liturgy**

Music: **Hollis Schachner**

Arranged by **Emily Tummons**
Piano arrangement and corresponding choral arrangement
by **Rachelle Nelson**

Corresponding choral arrangement available in *Kol Han'shamah: Choir Volume II* (TMP 994068)

F G C(add9) G/B Am F
Last time to Coda
Mel.
A-do-nai, tzu - ri v' - go - a - li, A-do-
optional solo instrument second time only
mp
1
2
Bass
Pno.
C B♭ G C G/B mf B Am
nai, tzu - ri v' - go - a - li. May the words of
optional solo instrument tacet first time
mf

Em F C F C G/B Am Em
20
Mel.
my mouth and the med - i - ta - tions of my
1
2
Bass
Pno.
Eb Bb G F G C Am
25
Mel.
heart be ac-cept - a-ble to You, A - do - nai,
1
2
Bass
Pno.

F C G(sus4) G
D.S. al Coda
Mel.
my Rock and my Re - deem - er. Yi- h'-
1
2
Bass
D.S. al Coda
Pno.

𝄌 CODA

Am A♭ C B♭ G
Mel.
go - - a - li, A - do - nai, tzu - ri v' - go - a -
1
2
Bass
Pno.

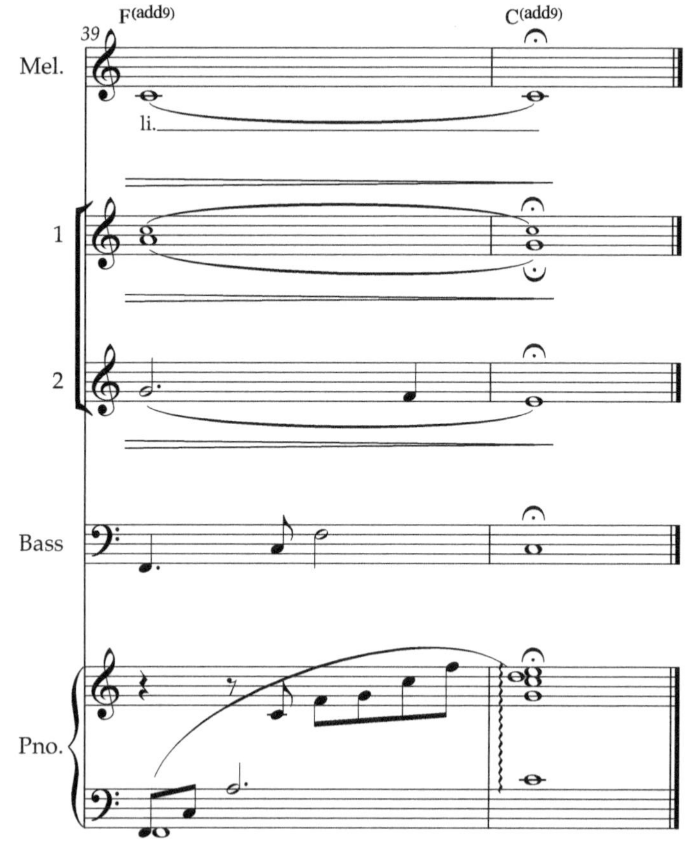

May the words of my mouth and the meditations of my heart
be acceptable to You, Adonai, my Rock and my Redeemer.

יִהְיוּ לְרָצוֹן אִמְרֵי פִי וְהֶגְיוֹן לִבִּי
לְפָנֶיךָ, יְיָ, צוּרִי וְגוֹאֲלִי.

Piano / Vocal

Yih'yu L'ratzon

יהיו לרצון

Text: **Liturgy**

Music: **Hollis Schachner**

Corresponding band arrangement by **Emily Tummons**
Piano arrangement and corresponding choral arrangement
by **Rachelle Nelson**

Corresponding choral arrangement available in *Kol Han'shamah: Choir Volume II* (TMP 994068)

C Bb G C G/B mf B Am
15
nai tzu - ri v'-go - a - li.
May the words of
mf
Em F C F C G/B Am Em
20
my mouth and the med - i - ta - tions of my
Eb Bb G F G C Am
25
heart be ac-cept - a-ble to You, A-do-nai,

F C G(sus4) G
D.S. al Coda
mp
my Rock and my Re-deem - er. Yi- h'-
D.S. al Coda
CODA
Am A♭ C B♭ G
mp
go - - a - li, A-do-nai, tzu - ri v'-go - a-
F(add9) C(add9)
li.

Lead Sheet / Melody for C Instruments

Yih'yu L'ratzon

יהיו לרצון

Text: **Liturgy**

Music: **Hollis Schachner**

Arranged by **Emily Tummons**

Melody for B♭ Instruments

Yih'yu L'ratzon

יהיו לרצון

Music: **Hollis Schachner**

Arranged by **Emily Tummons**

With deep passion; tenderly ♩ = 96

Corresponding choral arrangement available in *Kol Han'shamah: Choir Volume II* (TMP 994068)

Melody for E♭ Instruments

Yih'yu L'ratzon

יהיו לרצון

Music: **Hollis Schachner**

Arranged by **Emily Tummons**

With deep passion; tenderly ♩ = 96

Corresponding choral arrangement available in *Kol Han'shamah: Choir Volume II* (TMP 994068)

Melody for Bass Clef Instruments

Yih'yu L'ratzon

יהיו לרצון

Music: **Hollis Schachner**

Arranged by **Emily Tummons**

Corresponding choral arrangement available in *Kol Han'shamah: Choir Volume II* (TMP 994068)

Parts 1 and 2 for C Instruments

Yih'yu L'ratzon

יהיו לרצון

Music: **Hollis Schachner**

Arranged by **Emily Tummons**

With deep passion; tenderly ♩ = 96

Small notes indicate optional solo treble instrument

Corresponding choral arrangement available in *Kol Han'shamah: Choir Volume II* (TMP 994068)

994069

B
mf
mp
3
D.S. al Coda
CODA

Parts 1 and 2 for B♭ Instruments

Yih'yu L'ratzon

יהיו לרצון

Music: **Hollis Schachner**

Arranged by **Emily Tummons**

B
mf
mf
D.S. al Coda
mp
mp
CODA
mf
mf
mf
mp
mp
mp

Parts 1 and 2 for E♭ Instruments

Yih'yu L'ratzon

יהיו לרצון

Music: **Hollis Schachner**

Arranged by **Emily Tummons**

Corresponding choral arrangement available in *Kol Han'shamah: Choir Volume II* (TMP 994068)

B
mf
mp
D.S. al Coda
CODA

Bass

Yih'yu L'ratzon

יהיו לרצון

Music: **Hollis Schachner**

Arranged by **Emily Tummons**

Corresponding choral arrangement available in *Kol Han'shamah: Choir Volume II* (TMP 994068)

Full Score

Yism'chu

ישמחו

Text: **Shabbat liturgy**

Music: **Traditional Chasidic**

Arranged by **Emily Tummons**
Piano arrangement and corresponding choral arrangement
by **Robbie Solomon**

Corresponding choral arrangement available in *Kol Han'shamah: Choir Volume II* (TMP 994068)

F E Dm7 E F E Dm7 Dm F/C Bm7(b5) E
Mel.
shom - rei, shom - rei, shom - rei Shab - bat v' - ko - rei o - neg, Shab - bat.
1
2
Bass
Pno.
Rubato ♩ = ca. 92
B
E7 Am F B°/D E
1. Am m' - ka - d' - shei m' - ka - d'-shei sh' - vi - i, Shab - bat, ku-
(2.) i ra - tzi - ta bo, ra - tzi - ta bo v' - ki-dash-to, Shab - bat, chem
3. Zei - cher l' - ma - a - seih, l' - ma - a - seih v' - rei - shit, Shab - bat,
optional tacet Verse 1 and/or 2
mp
optional tacet Verse 1 and/or 2
mp

Tempo I
Am
Last time to Coda
Dm/F
Bm7(b5)
E
Mel.
lam yis - b' - u v' - yit - an - gu mi - tu - ve - cha, Shab - bat.
dat ya - mim o - to ka - ra - ta, Shab - bat.
zei - cher l' - ma - a - seih l' -
1
2
Bass
Pno.
C
F E Dm7 E F E Dm7
Yis - m' - chu v' - ma - l - chu - t' - cha shom - rei, shom - rei, shom - rei Shab - bat v'-
mf

27
Dm F/C Bm7(b5)
1. E
D.S.
2. E
D.S. al Coda
Mel.
ko-rei o-neg, Shab-bat. V'-hash-vi- Shab-bat.
1
2
Bass
Pno.
D.S.
D.S. al Coda

CODA

Tempo I
30
Dm/F Bm7(b5) E Bm7(b5)
D
E
Mel.
ma-a-seih v'-rei-shit, Sha-bat. Yis-m'-chu v'-ma-l-chu-t'-cha
1
2
Bass
Pno.
f

Those who keep Shabbat
by calling it a delight will rejoice in Your realm.
The people that hallow Shabbat
will delight in Your goodness.
For, being pleased with the Seventh Day,
You hallowed it as the most precious of days,
drawing our attention to the work of Creation.

יִשְׂמְחוּ בְמַלְכוּתְךָ
שׁוֹמְרֵי שַׁבָּת וְקוֹרְאֵי עֹנֶג.
עַם מְקַדְּשֵׁי שְׁבִיעִי,
כֻּלָּם יִשְׂבְּעוּ וְיִתְעַנְּגוּ מִטּוּבֶךָ.
וְהַשְּׁבִיעִי רָצִיתָ בּוֹ וְקִדַּשְׁתּוֹ,
חֶמְדַּת יָמִים אוֹתוֹ קָרָאתָ,
זֵכֶר לְמַעֲשֵׂה בְרֵאשִׁית.

Piano / Vocal

Yism'chu

ישמחו

Text: **Shabbat liturgy**

Music: **Traditional Chasidic**

Corresponding band arrangement by **Emily Tummons**
Piano arrangement and corresponding choral arrangement
by **Robbie Solomon**

Corresponding choral arrangement available in *Kol Han'shamah: Choir Volume II* (TMP 994068)

Rubato ♩ = ca. 92
B
E7 Am F B°/D E
1. Am m'-ka-d'-shei m'-ka-d'-shei sh'-vi-i, Shab-bat, ku-
(2.) i ra-tzi-ta bo, ra-tzi-ta bo v'-ki-dash-to, Shab-bat, chem
3. Zei-cher l'-ma-a-seih, l'-ma-a-seih v'-rei-shit, Shab-bat,
Am Last time to Coda Dm/F Bm7(b5) Tempo I E Bm7(b5)
lam yis-b'-u v'-yit-an-gu mi-tu-ve-cha, Shab-bat.
dat ya-mim o-to ka-ra-ta, Shab-bat.
zei-cher l'-ma-a-seih l'-
C
E F E Dm7 E F E Dm7
Yis-m'-chu v'-ma-l-chu-t'-cha shom-rei, shom-rei, shom-rei Shab-bat v'-

27
Dm F/C Bm7(b5)
1. E
D.S.
2. E
D.S. al Coda
ko - rei o - neg, Shab - bat. V'-hash- vi - Shab - bat.
D.S.
D.S. al Coda
CODA
Tempo I
30
Dm/F Bm7(b5) E Bm7(b5)
D
E
ma - a - seih v' - rei - shit, Sha - bat. Yis - m' - chu v' - ma - l - chu - t' - cha
34
F E Dm7 E F E Dm7 Bm7(b5) E
shom - rei, shom - rei, shom - rei Shab - bat v' - ko - rei o - neg, Shab - bat.

38
F E Dm7 E F E Dm7
Yis - m' - chu v' - ma - l - chu - t' - cha shom - rei, shom - rei, shom - rei Shab - bat v'-
42
Bm7(b5) E Bm7(b5) E
molto rit.
ko - rei o - neg, Shab - bat.
molto rit.

Lead Sheet / Melody for C Instruments

Yism'chu

ישמחו

Text: **Shabbat liturgy**

Music: **Traditional Chasidic**

Arranged by **Emily Tummons**
Corresponding choral arrangement by **Robbie Solomon**

Corresponding choral arrangement available in *Kol Han'shamah: Choir Volume II* (TMP 994068)

CODA
Tempo I
Dm Bm7(b5) E Bm7(b5) D E
30
ma - a - seih v' - rei - shit, Sha - bat. Yis - m' - chu v' - ma - l - chu - t' - cha
F E Dm7 E F E Dm7 Bm7(b5) E
34
shom - rei, shom - rei, shom - rei Shab - bat v' - ko - rei o - neg, Shab - bat.
F E Dm7 E F E Dm7
38
Yis - m' - chu v' - ma - l - chu - t' - cha shom - rei, shom - rei, shom - rei Shab - bat v'-
Bm7(b5) E Bm7(b5) E
42
molto rit.
ko - rei o - neg, Shab - bat.

Melody for B♭ Instruments

Yism'chu

ישמחו

Music: **Traditional Chasidic**

Arranged by **Emily Tummons**

Corresponding choral arrangement available in *Kol Han'shamah: Choir Volume II* (TMP 994068)

𝄌 *CODA*

Melody for E♭ Instruments

Yism'chu

ישמחו

Music: **Traditional Chasidic**

Arranged by **Emily Tummons**

Corresponding choral arrangement available in *Kol Han'shamah: Choir Volume II* (TMP 994068)

CODA

Melody for Bass Clef Instruments

Yism'chu

ישמחו

Music: **Traditional Chasidic**

Arranged by **Emily Tummons**

Corresponding choral arrangement available in *Kol Han'shamah: Choir Volume II* (TMP 994068)

𝄌 *CODA*

Parts 1 and 2 for C Instruments

Yism'chu

ישמחו

Music: **Traditional Chasidic**

Arranged by **Emily Tummons**

Corresponding choral arrangement available in *Kol Han'shamah: Choir Volume II* (TMP 994068)

Last time to Coda
Tempo I
19
23
C
Yism'chu...
mf
27
1.
D.S.
2.
D.S. al Coda

CODA
Tempo I
D
Yism'chu...
30
1
2
f
34
39
molto rit.

Parts 1 and 2 for B♭ Instruments

Yism'chu

ישמחו

Music: **Traditional Chasidic**

Arranged by **Emily Tummons**

Corresponding choral arrangement available in *Kol Han'shamah: Choir Volume II* (TMP 994068)

Last time to Coda
Tempo I
19
1
2
C
Yism'chu...
23
mf
27
1.
D.S.
2.
D.S. al Coda

CODA
Tempo I
Yism'chu...
D
molto rit.
molto rit.

Parts 1 and 2 for E♭ Instruments

Yism'chu

ישמחו

Music: **Traditional Chasidic**

Arranged by **Emily Tummons**

Corresponding choral arrangement available in *Kol Han'shamah: Choir Volume II* (TMP 994068)

Last time to Coda
Tempo I
C
Yism'chu...
mf
D.S.
D.S. al Coda

CODA
Tempo I
D
Yism'chu...
molto rit.
molto rit.

Bass

Yism'chu

ישמחו

Music: **Traditional Chasidic**

Arranged by **Emily Tummons**

Corresponding choral arrangement available in *Kol Han'shamah: Choir Volume II* (TMP 994068)